My Husband's a Woman Now

A Shared Journey of Transition and Love

Leslie Hilburn Fabian, LICSW

"My Husband's a Woman Now," by Leslie Hilburn Fabian, LICSW. ISBN 978-1-62137-431-2 (Softcover) 978-1-62137-432-9 (eBook)

Library of Congress Control Number: 2013922618.

Published 2014 by Virtualbookworm.com Publishing Inc., P.O. Box 9949, College Station, TX 77842, US. ©2014, Leslie Hilburn Fabian, LICSW. All rights reserved. No part of this publication may be reproduced, stored in a retrieval system, or transmitted in any form or by any means, electronic, mechanical, recording or otherwise, without the prior written permission of Leslie Hilburn Fabian, LICSW.

Manufactured in the United States of America.

CONTENTS

∞

DEDICATION

∞

To the memory of my parents, Edith Watrous Hilburn and John Presley Hilburn, who demonstrated how to accept being different and inspired me with their extraordinary love story.

To my amazing, magnanimous mother-in-law, Dorothy Crane Fabian, who has learned to accept and go with the flow.

To my beloved Deborah Rae Fabian—teaching me more about loving every day, by my side in every way.

AUTHOR'S NOTE

∽

SOME OF MY READERS MAY be seeking a model for traversing genderland paths similar to mine and my spouse's. If you are among them, I hope that you will glean strength and inspiration from this story. I've been urged by several astute friends and writing guides to include a compilation of what this experience has taught me, so I've added that as Part Four, "What This Experience Has Taught Me." Perhaps this will be of help to you in your own quest.

My Dear Fellow Spouses and Partners of Ts:

You may already have reacted to the title of this book. Before you read my story, I'd like to address some understandable areas of concern. I hope that I can be of help to you in some way.

What has happened in my life, what I have accepted and now live with, was not anticipated, prior to 2009. Despite twenty years of knowing I was married to a cross-dresser and of happily participating in many transgender adventures, I did not harbor the concern that my husband might someday want to become a woman. Our cross-dressing activities had seemed just that: Intermittent occasions for enjoying the camaraderie of others like us, for the fun of dressing-up, of playing-acting.

When you read this book, you will learn that I relished my male spouse's return to me after these events. That I am heterosexual. That I was in love with a man who had an unusual proclivity, which we both believed was as far as it needed to go. No harm in that. However, you will also read of my watching the devastation of my beloved upon resuming his male role. You may have experienced this with your own spouse.

I want to emphasize—as I say in the book—that my mate's anguish at the thought of wounding me, of "doing this to me," was probably as great as that of returning to his male self after dressing. I've explained that as he transitioned, he told me again and again, "I'll stop this immediately if it means losing you."

This is certainly not true of all transsexuals. Many reach the point of a complete inability to withstand remaining in their biological bodies. They proceed to transition, regardless of spouses' reactions or the havoc and pain they may be causing for others in their lives. We've all heard or read of this devastating circumstance. There are also those who never speak of their urgency to transition, for fear of the destructive results. They suffer in silence for the sake of maintaining the status quo.

I hope that this book, with its perspective of a spouse who's lived through her husband's transition and remained in the marriage, will provide some hope for others like us. There's no way to normalize the circumstance; no way to make it easy or more acceptable to others; no way to tell you that your life will be simple throughout and after a transition. You may live in fear that your husband or partner will eventually want to do as mine has done. And I am aware that you may despise me for allowing this in my marriage; for describing how it all came about, possibly providing encouragement to your spouse or partner in pursuing this end.

If so, this may not be the book for you. I strongly believe that each of us will find whatever stories we need to support our positions. However, I assert the following:

1. If you're married to a jerk, transitioning will only provide additional fodder for your anger, judgment, resentment, and pain. By deciding to transition, your spouse may be initiating the necessary process of ending an unsound relationship.
2. If your spouse is not a jerk, he may behave like mine, waiting decades to act on the need to transition. Mine would have chosen our relationship over the compulsion

to transition, should I have been unable to deal with it. Mine supported me every step of the way, as I have supported him (now her).

3. While you may grasp the depth of your spouse's need and find ways to accept and promote a transition, it may *not* work for you to remain in the relationship. However, it may be possible for you and your mate to create an end to your marriage with sensitivity, deep caring, and respect for your time together; for your family, your devotion, and your loving through the years.

To you who are willing to consider supporting this life-altering change, yet feel unable to remain in your relationship, please consider these questions:

1. Are you able to perceive the pain that this transsexual need has caused your mate?
2. Can you recognize how deep and intrinsic a part of him the need is? How long it's been present in your mate's life?
3. Is your partner caring and concerned about your well-being?
4. Might you devise, perhaps with outside help, ways to support a transition and travel this complicated path with your partner, while also exploring methods of changing or leaving the relationship?
5. Is there a way to remain loving toward one another as you traverse the difficult decisions?
6. Do you have resources to support yourself, such as friends, counselors, support groups, creative pursuits?

Perhaps the most important thing to remember is that *neither of you is bad or wrong!* You are human beings with human struggles—bigger than some, yet smaller than others. It seems to me that, in a human life, there are only degrees and variations of challenge, coupled with degrees and variations of resilience, reaction, and pain. *We have choices about everything.* This must be crystal clear, even if it's in recognizing that everything is on-hold for awhile, that we don't have the answers and may never have them, and that this is painful, almost beyond belief.

I would like to invite you to visit me at my website: www.lesliefab.com. I've been through it; I've survived it. In addition to remaining in my marriage, I'm a psychotherapist and coach, and I am ready to stand by you in plotting your own course through this perplexing transgender maze.

Blessings to you on your journey,

Leslie Hilburn Fabian

Dear Transgender Men (MTFs),

It is my hope that this book will inspire you to learn from the ways in which my husband handled his transition For months, he made it clear that he'd give-up his dream, if I couldn't remain in our marriage. You may feel unable to do this. I'd think it's rare that a transsexual might forego the process—at least once it's begun—for the sake of maintaining his marriage. I do not advise aspiring to this.

However, should you be married or partnered with a heterosexual woman and choose to transition, perhaps my experience will shed some light on what your spouse is going through, whether she's chosen to remain with you or not. Please understand that your transition is her transition as well; it alters her life irrevocably. It is not her dream-come-true; not something she was prepared to encounter or cope with in her life. Your becoming a woman makes her someone else, too, particularly if she should remain with you.

Of course, I'm sure that a huge component of your reluctance to proceed is knowing the pain you will inflict on your beloved by finally being true to yourself. Please consider that *neither of you is bad or wrong!* The ways in which you *handle* this situation is what can make it as good and right as possible, though I don't see that there's any way around the pain for both of you and those you love.

This does not sound particularly optimistic. Nevertheless, I maintain that this is a situation that can be endured and survived, sometimes with a marriage intact. I'm happy to add that we know other couples who've done it, as well!

My best wishes to you in finding your way to happiness, fulfillment, and acceptance,

Leslie Hilburn Fabian

∽∽

I am a Licensed Independent Clinical Social Worker. I came to the profession somewhat late in life, earning my Master's Degree in Social Work from Boston College at age forty-seven. Prior to that, I'd sat in the client's seat with a range of therapists through the years, working to understand and expunge my own inner demons. Because of this transformative work, I was inspired to become a psychotherapist myself, to assist others on the therapeutic path to well-being and health. For the record: When I feel the need for a helping hand, I continue to seek any and all manner of counseling, training, and support for myself, in whatever ways my life requires. For me, this is the healthiest way to live, and it's a commitment for my lifetime.

∽∽

In 1950, when I was one-year-old, my mother wrote in my baby book, "Leslie was born a happy baby and continues to be happy." Apparently, I'd begun life with a gift: An optimistic temperament. This joyful essence has been a constant blessing throughout my life. It serves me well and, I trust, enhances the lives of those whom I touch. I am grateful beyond words for this remarkable endowment.

PROLOGUE

∽

MY MOM, WHO DIED IN 2003, wrote brilliant letters. They were a joy to read after I'd moved from my childhood home, filled with intriguing narratives of her life with dad, current tales of the old neighborhood, and abundant adoration of me, my siblings, our spouses, and children. She'd actually aspired to write more than just family letters, excitedly gushing to me about snippets she'd jotted-down and kept tucking away for some future date. That date never came, however. Not because she died too soon, but because she always found some mundane activity more important than following her dream to write.

It would be natural to attribute her evasion of serious writing to paraplegia and her fifty-one years in a wheelchair, a result of polio at age twenty-nine. Or to raising four children, as my father climbed the corporate ladder. But once we kids were grown, my mother had abundant help and could have carved creative time from her life. No amount of urging on my part, however, seemed to penetrate her compulsion to have every detail of her life ordered before giving herself permission to write. Of course, she never succeeded in this impossible task.

So, in tribute to my mom, Edi Hilburn, and to honor my own aspirations in middle age, I began training myself to settle at the computer each morning, setting a timer for sixty minutes, then writing until the chime sounded. Often, after a quick break, I'd reset the timer and start again, eventually working-up to three-hour stints, minimum. This was particularly challenging, as I have Attention Deficit Hyperactivity Disorder [ADHD]!

As I began this routine at age sixty-one, I had yet to write my first book. Yet, I was determined to keep this commitment to myself as a top priority: To honor my creative expression and the possibilities of informing and entertaining others, perhaps even touching some hearts and souls along the way.

Among the countless blessings of my marriage is that my spouse supports me in running away from New England winters, to spend them in my native Florida. In 2010, I began an annual southward trek for warmth and creative solitude. After thirty years in Massachusetts, middle age had rendered me unwilling to continue enduring winters there, and I had no more excuses to keep me from my writing. My kids are grown; I'd put my work as a psychotherapist on hold; my honey supports me in every possible way. If these factors hadn't cleared the way for addressing my creative impulses, I figured I might just as well crawl into a hole!

Mary Oliver has written, *The most regretful people on earth are those who felt the call to creative work, who felt their own creative power restive and uprising, and gave to it neither power nor time.* I have answered the call, and this is my first literary offering.

When I began, I petitioned my deceased mother: "I know that you're in me, Mom—a gift in so many ways. But the part of you that wanted everything in order exists in me, too. If you are present now, in any form, I call on you to support me as I put aside every distraction and niggling thought or beckoning chore to write the book that you never did. I have things to say about this unusual life of mine." Here goes!

PREFACE

∞

WHEN MY HUSBAND DAVID was in transition to become a woman, I needed a vessel to contain the churning within me. Filling a daily journal page or two, as I'd done for decades, fell short of my overwhelming need to express myself and work through the process. I was the supportive, heterosexual wife of a male transsexual, transitioning to female. I had no guidelines.

As a Licensed Independent Clinical Social Worker and couple's therapist, I know that I *must* have my own working relationship, if I'm having one at all. For twenty years, I'd worked in tandem with my mate to build a joyful, fulfilling marriage. I still lacked a manual for handling this. The subject of transgenderism wasn't even mentioned in graduate school. Relationship books and workshops don't seem to touch it. So, getting this all into writing became the balm that soothed me and helped pave the way. It felt necessary for preserving my sanity.

Since the media has offered a multitude of transgender stories, books, interviews, and movies, I have not attempted to explain the phenomena of transexuality and transitioning. I've included a short glossary of terms for clarity, as this may be unfamiliar territory for some readers. However, this story is not clinical; it's a personal one, mine and ours alone.

In the early stages of my writing, prior to the transition in October 2011, a frequent challenge of putting the story into words was deciding what pronoun to use from sentence to sentence. I'd be writing about my husband David, then shift into talking about his femme alter, Deborah. I'd be speaking of Deb, only to drift into something regarding David.

I've done my best to refer to my spouse as "David" and "he" prior to the time of transition. When he was dressed as a woman, presenting as Deborah, and certainly since the transition to female, I've used the feminine name and pronoun. This semantic difficulty mirrors the intrinsic nature and complexity of the transition itself. Once David began consuming female hormones in the fall of 2009, there was nothing predictable or steady about my emotions.

Beyond the endeavor to handle my feelings, I began the book as a way of explaining one couple's journey through a strange conversion, one that few people will ever imagine. Soon after I'd begun, I realized that I wanted my husband's perspectives on what I was saying about the seismic change occurring in our lives. So, David began writing in response to what I'd produced, and this proved to be therapeutic for us both. Reading each other's literary efforts every few days brought us clarity and greater understanding of the other's process. For a while, this was a shared venture, a vehicle for discovering the depths of our love and ability to co-create.

Ultimately, I realized that this is *my* story about how the transition has affected *me,* so the book is nearly all mine. I've opted for a final section, the afterword, that is Debby's.

Two things are now unquestionable: we are closer to one another than ever before and we celebrate the active loving that infuses our relationship.

PART ONE
When I met my husband...

The Fabians, May 26, 1991

In all affairs it's a healthy thing now and then to hang a question mark on the things you have long taken for granted. –Bertrand Russell

∞

CHAPTER ONE
REALLY? DAVID FABIAN—IN A DRESS??

JOURNAL ENTRY: I know that my mate needs to look into more options for a feminine gender expression. I've said all along that I don't know what it will mean for us as a couple, if he decides to become Deborah to a greater extent. One thing is certain: My love for this exceptional being. But change is inevitable and I can't possibly know what lies ahead for us.

∞

"WHEN I MET MY HUSBAND, he was wearing a dress." I had occasionally made this surprising declaration during the first twenty years of my marriage to David. I'd been selective, of course, trusting my instincts to determine when and to whom it was safe to reveal this.

Making this bold pronouncement, I'd been "outing" my husband as a cross-dresser, exposing his life-long secret of sometimes wearing women's clothes. The statement was invariably shocking and confusing to others, but I had found it the least complicated, most direct way, of opening a conversation about who he truly was—or rather, who we thought he was.

Then, in 2009, after twenty-one years together, we both realized that David was more than "just a cross-dresser" and he began moving in a much more audacious direction. His sporadic feminine expression, the act of cross-dressing, had morphed into a plan to become a woman full-time. This revelation was alarming to the majority of people in David's life. They'd known him only as a man and it was unlikely they'd ever thought to question his undeniable masculinity, a perception based on observable details.

Some were aware that he had graduated from his Pennsylvania high school in 1967 as the scholar-athlete; that he'd gone on to the college of William and Mary in pre-med, playing soccer there. They may have known him as a scuba diver, a pilot, a man proficient at plumbing, electrical wiring, and building. They might have known that he served in the Navy, covering the costs of medical school at Hahnemann (now Drexel University), and that later he was a Marine Surgeon in the Reserves.

Most knew of David's three trips to Haiti as a volunteer after the 2010 earthquake; how he slept on the beach and operated in the most primitive of conditions. He'd been Chief of Surgery in one hospital and was the surgeon who welcomed a medical student from Scotland to his practice one summer, so that she could "shadow" and learn from him for six weeks. He'd been admired as a devoted father of four, an honorable man whose commitment to family had meant regular child support and alimony payments for over two decades.

All who knew David saw a skilled orthopedic surgeon, beloved and respected by hospital and office staff, patients, family, friends, and particularly by me, his wife. But the physical form, the skills, integrity, and brilliance of this individual—all that one could witness of his life—masked the inner workings of David R. Fabian, M.D.

∞

This transition story begins in middle age, in our early sixties. It is about the deconstructing of our previous life and the creation of a new one. My husband, David Robert Fabian, M.D., began living as a woman in the fall of 2011. This woman, Deborah Rae Fabian, has existed internally for all of David's remembered life.

My writing began about a year after female hormones entered David's bloodstream. I'd been restless the night before, with the 2010 Christmas holidays approaching. Awakening at

2:00 AM with thoughts racing, I first attributed the sleeplessness to my annual pre-holiday angst. But after running through every Christmas detail I could think of, I realized that my anxiety had deeper meaning. How interesting that, with the transition underway, I perceived my disturbance to be so superficial.

Just before going to sleep, I'd been reading Jonathan Mooney's *The Short Bus: A Journey Beyond Normal*. I realized that my reading material had stirred lots of feelings and began to wonder just how abnormal *I* was, encouraging David's transition. I was supporting what would inevitably be viewed as perverse or sick by some. In my willingness to go along with a change that might jeopardize our livelihood and well-being, I was also losing my husband in a most unusual way. I was distressed and confused about it.

Until late 2009, I'd had a husband who, with my approval, occasionally dressed and acted as if he were a woman. I'd go out with Deborah (David's femme name) for an evening or weekend get-away; then my husband returned to me. Most of the time we appeared to be an ordinary, heterosexual couple, despite a private, mostly-hidden life. Ultimately, it emerged that he would, forevermore, be a she. I'd no longer have a husband.

With all that had been churning in my conscious life and undoubtedly simmering on deeper levels, I wrote to survive this transition. I was incredibly sad when I began, for I loved the concept and reality of David, as my husband. Ironically, I also supported his right to be who he truly is. I have learned that paradox suffuses all of life; that I can hold two incongruous truths. This knowledge has sustained me as I've supported my beloved through his evolution—to her.

As the details of this journey are revealed, I hope that you will come to understand my perspective. What showed up is a love story of a rather extraordinary marriage—David's, Deborah's, and mine.

I am human, and nothing human is alien to me. –Terence

∽

CHAPTER TWO
WHAT IS GOING ON HERE?

JOURNAL ENTRY: I'm finally free from the confines of needing to be with a partner. I'm conscious of my daily choice to be with David, knowing full-well I am able to exist and flourish on my own. I relish the availability of this partner of mine and this delicious awareness of *wanting* rather than *needing* to be with him.

∽

IMAGINE HAVING A SECRET ABOUT YOURSELF, one so huge and shameful that you've hated it for as long as you can remember. So far, you've kept it at bay and have done everything right throughout your life: dressed acceptably, played sports, excelled in school, married your high school sweetheart. You've had children, become successful in your field—far surpassing average—and mastered a variety of skills and talents.

For all intents and purposes, your life appears ideal. But year after year, regardless of accomplishments and appearances, happiness eludes you. Eventually, you begin to know for certain: What stands in the way of satisfaction and joy is that dreadful secret which demands to be revealed, insisting to be acknowledged in some as-yet unknown way.

This scenario summarizes the first forty years of David's life. The pain and contempt for being transgender, of wishing he could be female, drove him nearly to suicide; and the impulse continued to plague him as we navigated the choppy waters of freeing Deborah.

For sixty years, he knew that his body was male. He'd represented his birth-gender admirably. But despite the male trappings, David's longing to be female had surfaced early in life. It was evident in his secret childhood yearning to play kickball with the girls. And he had loved their dresses, wishing for one of his own. Through his adult years, glancing at beautiful women had been from a longing—not to be *with* them, but to be one *of* them. This desire never abated, despite every conceivable effort to purge it.

David had denied all along that he felt like a woman trapped in a man's body, a common generalization regarding transsexuals. He had viewed this as a cliché, and derogatory, thereby spurning its application to who he was. Terrified of admitting that it might be true for him, his denial was maintained for decades. He had always known he had the right body for his XY chromosomal make-up; had never believed there had been a mistake, as many transsexuals do. It was just not the body that he wanted.

As he explained during the two-year transition from male to female, "My body just never meshed with my mind or my heart. I always figured I needed either a new brain or a new body. But I couldn't admit 'til now that I'm transsexual and allow myself to do something about the incongruity. For most of my life, I've just accepted that cross-dressing was as far as I'd go."

Many times through the years, David had told me he'd prefer to live as a woman full-time, if only it were feasible. I doubt he believed it could ever be so, and I'd always seen it as a pipedream, unlikely ever to manifest. Now this elusive fantasy has become a reality.

After six decades of angst, self-loathing, and an unrelenting inner battle, the feminine in David finally prevailed. Whatever stood in the way of this choice—first wife, children, parents, colleagues, medical practice, fear—all prohibited him from being true to him- or, rather, *her*self. Now, in this stage of our lives, with children grown and the allure of retirement ever closer, Deborah is finally living her truth.

Inevitably, you will ask what I, the wife of a transsexual, can possibly gain from this transition. It's a reasonable question, one that concerned friends asked me many times. It dogged me and begged to be answered.

Alas, as with so many of life's questions, there may be no clear, adequate, sustainable response. One might ask the spouse or partner of an individual with cancer; with aids or a disfigurement; a disability, perhaps, or mental illness, "What keeps you married to this person?"

Is it adequate to say, "I love her," or "He needs me," or simply, "We belong together?" I think the reasons are always personal; a choice, whether conscious or not, that each of us makes in relationship, regardless of circumstances.

Years ago, I *consciously* determined that I'd be married to this person as a *choice*, not out of need or habit, or even because of the certificate that establishes our legal status. As my story will tell, we've had more than our share of challenges and uncertainty. Many factors challenged my commitment to this marriage from time to time. Yet our marriage remains an on-going work-in-progress; a project in living two lives together—joyfully.

Every heart whispers a song, incomplete, until
another heart whispers back. –Plato

CHAPTER THREE
AS FATE WOULD HAVE IT

JOURNAL ENTRY: I've met the most intriguing, unusual man at the Floating Circle. He was wearing women's clothes! It didn't seem to matter though. I saw (and felt) something that's incredibly attractive to me. When we said goodbye, I knew I'd see him again, though I have no idea how that might happen. Funny. I can't help but think of him as a HIM, even though Niela corrected me when I said I was attracted to "him." It's just so clear to me that he's an amazing man, albeit with a rather strange presentation!

Surprisingly, we met at my women's group in 1987—and it was Deborah I first met, not David. He'd been invited, along with three other Ts [transgendered individuals], as a special guest, to help us explore the question, "What is a Woman, Anyway?"

This group had begun gathering in 1986, then met for seventeen years. We called it "The Women's Floating Circle," since we traveled each month to a different member's home in the Boston-area. We would first share a potluck meal, schmoozing and catching-up on each other's lives. Then we'd focus on our monthly topic, pre-determined by the hostess, with each of us, in turn, sharing her story related to the theme.

Our holiday gathering of 1987 had promised to be memorable. Niela, the group's founder and a psychotherapist, was holding the December event in her home and calling it "Women in Genderland." There was high anticipation regarding the topic, as she's an expert in the field of transgenderism. The rest of us then knew very little about this subject.

Niela had extended our usual four-hour format by two hours, since she'd invited these four former clients to join us for dessert. They'd agreed to come, to answer questions and increase our paltry knowledge of the topic. Our guests would include a postoperative male-to-female transsexual, two cross-dressers (one was Deborah, not then aware that she was transsexual), and an androgynous individual. Obviously, there was no possible way I could have known how this event would alter my life.

Remembering the occasion invariably brings me back to the raw edges of grief I was feeling at the time. Just five months earlier on the Fourth of July, my only sister had taken her life. This had been my second struggle to accept the loss of a sibling to suicide. My younger brother had killed himself fourteen years earlier. In my extreme sorrow, I was grateful beyond measure for the security and support I felt with my women's group, whose members were primarily psychotherapists.

Despite the unusual appearances and stories that we heard from all of Niela's guests that evening, it was Deborah's tale that drew me in. As the details emerged, I felt some part of myself opening, my numbness begin to diminish. Deborah was entering my life.

We'd been invited by Niela to ask our visitors anything, though they were at liberty not to respond, if a query was too uncomfortable. I'd been impressed by Deborah's straightforward replies to all questions posed. Though she seemed apologetic about the desire to dress, it was clear that the urge was irresistible, and I marveled at her wish to be known in her most vulnerable state.

Here sat a rather large man wearing a deep-purple dress, jewel-toned scarf, tasteful makeup. The hair (a wig) was carefully coiffed. Dark pantyhose and black heels completed the visage. I admired this individual's desire to become known in his—rather, *her*—authenticity. With a room full of strangers, he was sharing his female persona for the first time ever, and what most attracted me were the courage and honesty I witnessed that day.

We learned that David had cross-dressed since early adolescence, but always in private and with devastating after-effects. Yet, despite the pervasive shame and self-loathing that resulted, the compelling desire was ever-present, awaiting another opportunity to express itself. Pleasure in the act was fleeting, and consistent happiness had been an elusive dream for decades.

Finally, approaching forty, David had realized he could no longer stand being miserable. Desperate for relief, he'd found Niela, and her therapeutic assistance was allowing him to permit the feminine to emerge. Now, here was Deborah in all her glory, sharing herself with the world—or at least a very small part of it.

It's been fascinating to recall how differently David and I experienced this event. My overriding perception of him was one of bravery and forthrightness; of a sweet vulnerability in admitting to us, "I don't know why I do this. I've tried for years to make it go away. I only know that I have to do it and I almost always have."

His account of our meeting paints an entirely different story. In his indelicate words, he'd been "scared shitless." A mutual attraction to me had triggered an intense fear of humiliation and embarrassment. Fortunately, these feelings didn't stand in the way of an affectionate hug at the end of the evening.

∽⚮∽

We'd not met in a vacuum, of course. We were both thirty-eight, but lived in extremely different circumstances. I'd been divorced for six years and was raising my two kids alone. Then fifteen and twelve, they saw their father infrequently; he'd moved to the South when we'd split and made little effort to be with them. My finances consistently challenged me. I'd obtained my undergraduate degree in human services a few years before and was attempting to be a good mom, run a business of my own, and maintain a sales job as well. I'd been open to a relationship. In fact, in my on-going efforts to improve my life, I'd formulated a list of what I wanted in a man.

Since the guys I'd been dating were clueless in the realm of effective parenting and what that required, I was determined that any long-term partner of mine would be as dedicated to his kids as I was to my own. But in compiling my list, I'd foolishly omitted specifics about how many children the man might have or what their ages should be. I had also neglected to specify that he be comfortable in his masculinity. Who would think to add a statement regarding how the man should feel about being a man?

Another huge oversight concerned the availability of my ideal partner. This should have topped the list, but I'd unwisely taken it for granted. Ironically, I'd been adamant in my life, even verbalizing to friends, "I could never be the other woman. I like women too much to do that." Surprise! It turned out that David was married. The Floating Circle narrative had included mention of a wife, a lousy marriage, and a twelve-year-old daughter. Perhaps from wishful thinking, I'd assumed this was the extent of the family.

As I'd realized my attraction to this individual, feeling captivated by her honesty and vulnerability, I was even more intrigued when she'd told us, "I'm an orthopedic surgeon."

I remember thinking, "Really? There are successful, working people who do this?" (Like most people in 1987, I was incredibly naïve about the abundance of transgender individuals in the world, in all walks of life.)

Despite the female attire and marital status (and Deborah had sounded as if she was on the verge of ending the marriage), the entire package had drawn me in. By the end of the evening, when I thanked her and we hugged, I was smitten. Gazing into those aquamarine eyes, I somehow knew for certain that we'd see each other again. Deborah departed and I raced into my friend's kitchen blurting, "Oh my God, Niela! I'm so attracted to him!"

She'd turned to me with a sardonic grin. "You mean *her*, don't you, Leslie?"

The pronoun conundrum had begun. And there was more irony here: It had apparently made no difference to me, unquestionably heterosexual, that I was wildly attracted to a man in a dress. Despite her presentation and accompanying story, I had seen Deborah not as an effeminate man in drag, but as an intriguing man expressing an unusual need. Had I perceived that he was effeminate, it's unlikely there'd have been an attraction— I'd always been drawn to masculine men. The pull was to an essence far beneath the feminine trappings. Something deep within her had touched me to the core.

*You can't reason with your heart; is has its own laws and thumps
about things which the intellect scorns. –Mark Twain*

CHAPTER FOUR
NOW WHAT?

JOURNAL ENTRY: I was totally out of my mind, attempting to
seduce David. I desperately wanted to make love! Thank God
I'm mindful again, realizing that being with him behind his
wife's back (his WIFE, Leslie!) is not on my agenda. I've got my
integrity back—my ability to decide what's right, regardless of
my overwhelming desire for him. But how long will I wake up
looking for him, reaching for him, dreaming of holding him—and
wondering whether he's dreaming of and wanting me, too?

SOON AFTER MEETING DEBORAH, I was off with my kids for the
1987 Christmas holidays, visiting my folks in my hometown
Tampa, Florida. I'd always been able to share practically
anything with my open-minded mom, so of course, I revealed the
story of The Floating Circle gathering. She was as fascinated as I.
I was also candid about my attraction to the tall, thin man in the
purple dress. Little did we know that within three years "she"
would be my husband.

My kids and I returned to Massachusetts to tackle winter in
New England, always daunting for this Florida native. To ease
my way through the season, I'd signed-up for a five-month
workshop called "The Living Soul" which began early in 1988. It
was another creation of my friend Niela, and would include
Jungian dream-work, soulful artistic expression, and a variety of
exercises to take participants deeper into their own souls. We
would meet once a month through May.

The first all-day event began on a Saturday morning early in the new year. As soon as I arrived, I noticed a lanky man across the room, immediately recognizable as Deborah—in male mode. It was David this time; we would both be Living Soul participants. I'd thought, *Oh my God, there he is! I knew I'd see him again.*

Before the class began, Niela asked the two of us to copy some hand-outs, giving us a brief opportunity to reconnect at the copy machine. "Do you recognize me?" David asked anxiously.

"Of course I do! You're Deborah!"

I was thrilled to rediscover this person, just a month after our initial meeting. I also noticed that David's male persona definitely appealed to me. It seemed almost too good to be true!

During the brief copy-making task, I began to learn additional details of David's life and to share some of mine with him. One thing he revealed that January morning was that his family was larger than I'd presumed. Though he'd previously mentioned his twelve-year-old, he actually had four children, under the age of thirteen. Naturally, I was stunned.

He also revealed that, despite the dreadful status of his sixteen-year marriage, he was not on the cusp of leaving it. For some time, he'd been attempting to save it, though this appeared to be a losing battle. It sounded as if he was expected to make all the changes and accommodations, much as my former husband had demanded of me. David was blamed for all of their problems, with cross-dressing (which his wife had discovered, but never witnessed) topping the list.

It was soon clear that the allure between us was mutual and deep. After seven hours of working together with the group, we ended the day speaking candidly about our attraction, both of us expressing disdain for anything elicit. Cross-dressing was never mentioned; it seemed to have receded into an irrelevant void. What we felt for each other was compelling and primal, yet we were totally perplexed by what to do about our feelings.

The next afternoon David called me. (My number was readily available, as workshop participants had all agreed to exchange contact information.) "I can't stop thinking about you. I could hardly sleep last night, and I can't eat," he told me. "Is there any chance we can meet, to talk about this?"

I'd heard men's lines before and this sure as hell sounded like one! But he seemed so sincere—sensitive and vulnerable in the ways that had first appealed to me when I'd met him as Deborah. Curiosity outweighed my hesitation and I agreed to meet him for lunch in a couple of days. Apparently, I thought myself capable of conducting a simple discussion of those raw, primal feelings we were both experiencing. The transgenderism had become either immaterial or simply forgotten by me. I was smitten—and, clearly, so was he.

What ensued was a lunch with sparks flying. I remember David's knee touching mine at one point, and it seemed as if an electrical current flowed between us. I doubt we resolved anything that day about how to proceed, but it was clear that resisting each other would be next to impossible.

As The Living Soul continued, we saw each other sporadically between monthly gatherings. David would leave his orthopedic office for psychotherapy sessions with Niela in the town where I lived, and we'd meet for breakfast or go for a walk after his session. We were unconcerned about being observed by people who knew him, as this was some distance from his home. Deborah did not reappear, and thoughts of David's transgenderism continued to recede for me. For the time being, cross-dressing was his own private affair.

During the five anxious months of our meetings, we discovered what is meant by "an affair of the heart." Gazing into each other's eyes, we had felt like lovers, though consistently maintaining our physical boundaries. Neither of us would allow long, stolen kisses to go any further. Yet, we felt joined to one another in inexplicable ways. We exchanged cards and letters; he sent me flowers and gifts. I was clearly being wooed.

While blatantly ignoring my principles, I still fought to maintain my sensibility, knowing that David might never free himself to be with me. As I listened to his litany of woes, I'd wonder how he could stay in the marriage after years of such unhappiness. Then he'd reiterate his concerns for his highly dependent wife, the distressing thought of leaving his children, his apprehension about friends and his medical practice. It became clear that David's modus operandi included denying his own satisfaction and desires, while attempting to ensure everyone else's.

I, too, felt concern for the hurt that his leaving would inflict. I told him again and again, "Do not leave your wife for me. If you're going to do it, you have to do it for yourself—not for what you think we'll have together. There's no guarantee for us."

As May approached and we neared the end of The Living Soul, I was becoming anxious. I advised myself repeatedly, "He may never leave her, Leslie. Prepare yourself to end this."

I told this married man that I'd soon abolish him from my life unless he freed himself to be with me. I made it clear that I would not wait indefinitely for him to be available. And I geared-up for another loss. A close woman friend told me to call her at any hour of the day or night, in an effort to assist me through those moments when I could barely resist contacting him.

The final day of the workshop arrived, a sad one for all twelve participants. The months of working together, of building connections and sharing our deepest selves, meant a loss for everyone. So, we planned a reunion for June. Of course, this meant a welcome delay to what now seemed inevitable: My terminating the (apparently) dead-end relationship with David.

I volunteered my home for our gathering and we assembled for pot-luck, sharing our challenges and successes from the previous weeks. For me, the air was charged with unfulfilled sexual tension and the exhilaration of being with my beloved again. Ultimately, everyone but David departed and I threw caution to the wind, luring him into my bedroom. After a month's separation, it appeared that adultery was not beyond me. I figured that he was the one who'd have to deal with the consequences at home, and I could no longer resist my body's longing.

As it turned out, humility slammed me that night. Despite groveling together on the bed for a while and my literally begging him to make love to me, *the man resisted.* I'd never before doubted my seductive abilities, but that night David's integrity ruled. He finally tore himself away from me, fully clothed and virtuous, leaving me thwarted—and alone again.

Never let the odds keep you from doing what you know in your heart you were meant to do. –H. Jackson Brown, Jr.

∞

CHAPTER FIVE
NEW CHOICES, BIG CHANGE

JOURNAL ENTRY: David told me in July that he knew we'd be together someday. I felt it, too, and could actually picture us growing old together—but I wasn't sure he'd make it happen and it was all up to him. I had to be strong and smart and take care of myself first.

∞

Throughout The Living Soul, I had been telling David about Insight Seminars, a series of personal growth workshops that I'd been involved in for a couple of years. He'd seemed hungry for more awareness and expansion, as his self-knowledge and growth had intensified in The Living Soul; and I was eager to share the experience with anyone who would listen and consider attending, since my life had improved immeasurably through my Insight work. I viewed sharing it as a way for individuals to change themselves, thereby changing the planet for the better.

He signed-up for the July, 1988 seminar, "The Awakening Heart," and I decided to audit the training. I knew that I was simply delaying the inevitable, but I felt desperate to be near him. Nevertheless, I was determined to stop the seemingly dead-end relationship as soon as the workshop ended.

During the seminar, I witnessed David's transformation. I watched a man who'd been sorrowful, confused, and self-deprecating adopt an entirely new set of positive beliefs and expectations. Early experiences in life had prepared him to anticipate negativity and accept it, never questioning his unhappiness; yet, this distortion dropped-away in the seminar. He began to understand that life can be joyful, fulfilling, and a good deal more. He'd glimpsed ways to create an existence that might actually be filled with love, satisfaction, meaningful communication, and openness. The Insight training seemed to catapult David into choosing happiness as a new way of living.

Of course, as soon as the workshop ended, there was no viable reason to continue seeing him. He was still married and I was no longer willing to continue the charade, waiting in the wings. It was time to accept that our deep connection and my joy in witnessing his new-found sense of freedom would become only beautiful memories. Though it felt as though my heart would break, I had to purge him from my life.

Just prior to the Insight Seminar, I'd sent my son south to live with his dad—another huge loss—and I needed to get away for awhile. I decided that a vacation was in order. I would cut-off communication with David, not letting him know where I'd be. This had seemed vital to my mental and emotional well-being; a way to sever the ties and resume my life without him.

My daughter, now fifteen, invited a girlfriend and the three of us took off for a week in the Pennsylvania mountains, heading for an old family place where I'd spent most of my childhood summers. Since the owners, my great aunt and uncle, had passed-away and the property was still in the family, we'd have the place to ourselves.

This was before the advent of cell phones, so I was able to leave home, reachable only by those who knew the phone number of the old farmhouse—my parents, former husband, and a couple of friends. It had felt liberating, taking this time away, with no possibility of David's calling me. But, ironically, just after our departure, he reached the limit of trying to save his miserable marriage. He could no longer deny and contort himself, in an effort to satisfy his wife's needs and demands.

For months before this, he'd told me that, if and when he left her, he'd be at my doorstep in a heartbeat. I'd loved hearing this, though I'd barely entertained the possibility of its happening. Then everything changed. He'd left his wife and, true to his word, began trying to find me, knowing only that I was somewhere in the sprawling state of Pennsylvania!

Early in the morning after our arrival at the farm, I was jolted awake by the ringing of the downstairs telephone. Half asleep and alarmed by a call at 2:00 AM, I ran down the stairs to answer it. I'd been astonished to hear David's voice, telling me he'd left his wife, and that he was somewhere in New York state. He had been on his way to find me. Then, stressed and rushing late into the night, he'd fallen asleep at the wheel of his car and had totaled it! After assuring me he was unharmed, he said that he'd checked into a hotel for a few hours' sleep and would continue his quest in a rental car later that morning.

As thrilled as I was with this news and the confirmation that he was unhurt, I began to feel annoyed, wondering how he'd found me. "I called information and got your parents' number," he said. "I knew your dad's name and he was the only one listed, so I called."

"Your mom gave me the farmhouse number and told me you're in Muncy Valley, but I can't find it on the map. I found Muncy, so that's where I was headed. Are they close together?"

At this point, I became overwhelmed by the significance of what David was telling me. The man had been pursuing me for seven months, incapable of making up his mind. Now, as promised, he was headed for my doorstep in a place he couldn't even find on the map. I was annoyed that my mother had given him the phone number without my okay, since I'd intended to be inaccessible to him. But my anger started slipping-away as it began to sink in that David was now free to be with me!

I don't recall sleeping much the rest of that night. It was exhilarating to know that my beloved was now available; that he was unhurt after wrecking his car and would soon to be on my doorstep. He arrived mid-morning and we had the sweetest of reunions. Banishing the girls from the house, we finally acted on months of thwarted passion—to our great pleasure, joy, and wonder.

Shortly thereafter, I was shocked again. David informed me he'd be there for only one day. He'd promised his kids he'd be back for his birthday, two days away. I was stunned that I'd lose him so quickly when, *finally*, we were free to be together.

But I was grateful we'd have twenty-four hours of bliss. I consoled myself with the awareness that here was the devoted father I'd been seeking in a mate.

Let there be spaces in your togetherness and
let the winds of heaven dance between you. –Kahlil Gibran

∞

CHAPTER SIX
THE MAN OF MY DREAMS

JOURNAL ENTRY: My whole life feels like a celebration now! I'm simply shocked sometimes with the sheer pleasure and joy of it. I just don't know that David ever feels as joyful and free as I do. He can't seem to allow this into his life—even though we are finally together.

∞

After seven months of desire, distress, and longing, we still did our damndest to uphold some modicum of integrity, with regard to David's wife. We refrained from moving in together for awhile, as it seemed prudent and kind to wait until their divorce was final. I was also unwavering in my belief that he spend some time living alone, as I know the propensity of human beings to move rapidly from one dysfunctional relationship into another.

After seven years on my own, wholly committed to my self-discovery and expansion, I felt it was essential that a life partner also know himself well, with a continuing desire for self-examination and growth. I hoped that he'd take the time to heal and to know himself better.

In 1990, with David's divorce complete, we acted on our longing to live together. We were forty-one when we bought and moved into a house of our own. It was a twenty-minute drive from David's children, who were shuttled back and forth between their mother's home and ours, and close enough for David to attend most of their games and activities. My own kids were out of the nest, my daughter at a Boston college and my son in the South with his dad.

Soon after settling into our home, before I'd decided to attend graduate school and become a psychotherapist, I began a new job in sales. The position entailed traveling and remaining for several weeks at the hotel or resort where I was working. For the first time in my life, I was on my own.

This felt extraordinary, as I'd been married at twenty and raising children for eighteen years. I loved the independence and freedom. On these business trips, there were no meals to cook, mail to open, bills to pay. While away, I had nothing to think of but me and my exciting, new career. I even had maid service!

Then, shortly after I began traveling, a friend had asked me, "Well, Leslie, now that you've found the man of your dreams, what's it like going off and leaving him for weeks at a time?"

I'd been taken-aback by this question, since I hadn't hesitated for a moment to take the job. Despite now living with my beloved David, I *was* running off by myself for extended periods of time, and I began to ponder the implications of this logical query.

True, after seven single years, I had found the man of my dreams. David was precisely the mate I'd longed for, despite being married, the father of four young children, and wearing women's clothes when we'd met. He was kind, loving, attentive, and a great dad, devoted to his children. He'd even been determined to ensure his former wife's security and comfort, as well as that of his kids. And drawn, as I was, to self-observation and change, I loved that he worked with me to resolve whatever difficulties arose in our new life together. He was, indeed, the man of which I'd dreamed. Even so, I was leaving him for weeks at a time, working at my job, and reveling in my new-found autonomy.

Reflecting on my friend's question, I began to realize the extent of my own healing and self-actualization. I was now assured and capable, able to stand on my own. I also recognized that David was the kind of partner who wanted the best for me, just as I desired that for him. I came to see that this man was loving me as much and as well as I loved him, and this felt truly miraculous!

Naturally, my weeks away made for happy reunions, which we both anticipated with excitement, albeit with somewhat different expectations. Envisioning the pleasures of sizzling sex and sweet nights of cuddling, each of us looked forward to sexy women's lingerie—with David picturing himself in his own lacy frills! This was not quite what I had in mind, though I learned to expect and prepare myself for it. After-all, he'd been dressed as a woman when we'd met, though I'd not known, in the beginning, that this would extend to our sex life.

At first, the excitement of exploring each other sexually was delicious in every way, regardless of what we wore. Satisfaction was rarely an issue; we were madly in love and overjoyed that we were now lovers. I could happily accommodate my partner's cross-dressing—even in the bedroom, *most* of the time. My flexibility and willingness to fulfill David's fantasies felt like a gift to my beloved, and I received much in return.

Though heterosexual without question, I do love fantasy. So, I found it easy, for awhile, to encourage David in pretending to be the woman he envisioned. Sometimes though, before returning from my travels, I'd ask to be greeted and bedded by David, the man. He'd agree, though this seemed to dampen his ardor, eliciting fears that I was no longer willing to participate in his cross-dressing—or that I wanted him to stop it completely.

Considering the newness of our connection and years of David's self-judgment and fear, this was understandable. However, it simply was not the case. I'd merely been asking for what I wanted, for a change. I began to notice that my partner often seemed to view things in black and white, especially concerning this sensitive issue. His mindset contrasted sharply with my penchant for seeing life in many shades of gray.

When we'd been together for about five years, David became active with the Reserves. Since I was no longer traveling in my work and am passionate about my solitude, I looked forward to the times he'd go off for his two weeks of active duty. I also relished the expectation of our joyful reunions. But, unrealistically, as his two weeks wound-down, I'd picture this man of my dreams—my Marine Surgeon husband—returning in uniform, anxious to make mad, passionate love to me. In the mind of the homecoming soldier, however, the image and desire were oh, so different! After two rough-and-tumble weeks in the desert, of sharing quarters with other men and hiding his secret self, David wanted nothing more than to return to me, put on a nightgown, and settle into the banished guise of Deborah.

Our divergent expectations and the resulting frustration began to wear on me. Getting what I wanted in the sexual realm—for him to pretend (since that's what it took, apparently) that he was an amorous, masculine man—became a fairly consistent disparity. The actual event was often fraught with disappointment, and the struggle proved to be one of our most painful and challenging through our early years together.

I longed for something other than his fantasy of feigned femininity. Occasionally, I wanted more traditional roles in the bedroom, and kept encouraging him to take this initiative. But this sometimes resulted in deep heartache for both of us.

Throughout these times, David rarely ceased in his longing to be a woman. When he returned from those two weeks with the Marines. a rigorous day of patients and surgery, or a weekend as a highly-involved soccer-hockey-skiing dad, he could finally "let his hair down," figuratively *and* literally. He wanted to be Deborah more than anything else. This often included a passionate desire to make love with me, though shifting back into feeling masculine was the last thing on his mind.

Regardless of what happened in our bedroom, I generally forgot about Deborah's existence, once David's male persona reemerged. He'd leave for the office and my thoughts during the day were of my husband, the *man* I loved, not a man pretending to be a woman. I loved his masculine expression, his seeming comfort with the many ways in which he appeared to be a "real man." I believed I'd found the perfect mate who simply had an unusual proclivity, one that I was more than willing to indulge, some of the time. In fact, most of the time I was committed to supporting his desire to express his extreme feminine side, just as he reinforced many of my whims and endeavors. I rarely entertained delusions of changing him, other than seeking more variation in our sex life.

It was fun to support our evening or weekend forays as Deborah and Leslie. I'd done my best to deal with David's need to be Deborah in the bedroom, assuring him that my desire for something different was neither a request nor a demand that Deborah disappear. I hoped he'd relax into trusting this. Our love and commitment grew; our foundation of authenticity and deep connection expanded.

We had other challenges, of course, as every couple has. Besides those in the sexual realm, our differences in the management of children were particularly problematic. But I'd found a partner with whom I could discuss and resolve whatever came up. Gradually, we both felt safer, more loved, more loving, in spite of some robust disagreement. Oftentimes, we'd simply agree to disagree, knowing that our bond could withstand this divergence of opinions. And, since David's children were not mine, we eventually determined that he'd have the final say about them. I learned to detach from the parenting issues, leaving these up to him and their mother.

What has delighted me as we've aged are the countless ways in which we feel close, beyond overt sexual expression. My first marriage had been all about the physical—our attraction, the frequent sex, procreation. While David and I had plenty of sex in our early years together, we've relished much physical closeness and intimacy of other kinds: Touching often, holding hands as we stroll or during meals, in deep discussion, traveling, snuggling in bed.

What became far more important than the sexual demonstration of our love were these many other intimate expressions that came forward. It was as though we'd realized what's missing when an immature relationship runs the initial course of physical attraction and hot sex. We were developing those dimensions of relationship beyond sexual intimacy, calling for self-awareness, flexibility, maturity, generosity, patience, and the ability to stand alone when necessary.

We have respected and supported each other, doing our best to understand when either of us feels hurt or frustrated. And we've practiced forgiveness and listening *intently* as much as possible. Discussions concerning kids' issues, or anything else that has arisen, have rarely failed to deepen our understanding and mutual support, even when they've begun in disagreement.

We had already delved deeply within ourselves before we met, far surpassing the negligible self-knowledge of our early adult years. There was simply more depth and intimacy to share with one another, superseding the compelling need for frequent sexual expression.

A conscious relationship is not a sometime thing....
Our commitment must be indelible and steadfast; something our
partner can rely upon. –Harville Hendrix and Helen Hunt

∞

CHAPTER SEVEN
CAN THIS MARRIAGE WORK?

JOURNAL ENTRY: Sometimes I get so frustrated! I feel such playfulness and desire, but David can't or won't join me in this. He seems wrapped-up in whatever veil surrounds him and it's impenetrable, at times—I just can't get him to connect. Then, other times, he realizes how far away he's gone and shows me how much he needs and loves me, with all the tenderness that was there in the beginning. Where does my playmate go when I'm here, wanting so much to share all of me with him; wanting him to be with me in this joy? I just don't understand.

∞

DESPITE THE SEXUAL CHALLENGES and our combined family of six kids—aged nineteen to four—of huge alimony and child support payments and the tribulations of dealing with former spouses, we were married on our front lawn on May 26, 1991. We'd already worked hard on the relationship, and there was no doubt that we belonged together. But we knew that smooth sailing was probably unlikely for us.

One vital step we had taken prior to moving-in together had been reading Harville Hendrix and Helen Hunt's *Getting The Love You Want*. From working through the exercises therein, we'd discovered much about what had drawn us together, what caused issues to arise, and how to assist each other in resolving our differences. We determined that ours would be what Hendrix and Hunt label a "conscious relationship." This means ...*committing to understanding our own wounds and those of our partner, to learning new skills and changing our hurtful behavior, in the course of which we [would] meet our partner's needs and restore the lost and denied parts of ourselves, thus achieving spiritual wholeness.*[1] We came to believe we might actually get the love that each of us sought in a healthy, mature, and fulfilling relationship.

The most profound, tangible outcome of our efforts with the Hendrix/Hunt material was what is called a "relationship vision," the result of one of the exercises. Our list of nineteen positive affirmations became the foundation of our bond to one another. Each component of the vision was eventually incorporated into our wedding vows and we've attempted to live them as best we can. We still see this vision daily; it's framed and hanging in our home:

> ➢ We are totally honest with each other
> ➢ We trust each other
> ➢ We are each other's best friend
> ➢ We make time to laugh and play
> ➢ We are committed to spiritual expansion and exploration
> ➢ We are effective and loving parents, supporting each other in the presence of our children
> ➢ We support and encourage each other's growth and healing
> ➢ We take time to be alone
> ➢ We listen and speak from our hearts
> ➢ We have frequent exciting and fulfilling sexual unions
> ➢ We respect each other's personal time and space
> ➢ We are open to change
> ➢ We support each other's career goals and aspirations
> ➢ We share important decisions
> ➢ We are healthy and physically active
> ➢ We are financially secure and prepared for life-long financial security
> ➢ We resolve our differences quickly and with ease
> ➢ We create win-win solutions
> ➢ We are sharing a beautiful home filled with love, laughter, and joy

---

[1] *The Couples Companion*, Pocket Books, NY, NY, 1994.

Reviewing these statements some two decades after first visualizing and creating our relationship, I am amazed at how clearly we knew what we wanted in our life together; how compelled we were, with our two failed marriages, to make ours the best it could be. We have sometimes strayed from these guidelines, of course. But when this happens, one of us will eventually spout a line from the vision, a reminder that whatever ugliness or struggle has arisen is not part of our intention as a couple. Then the work begins, with dedication to our vision and our resolve, to bring us back to our loving.

One summer I participated in a professional workshop for therapists, led by Harville Hendrix and three of his trainers. I had taken our vision with me to show Dr. Hendrix and was asked to read it aloud in the seminar. It was an honor to share the vision that makes our marriage extraordinary, and it was poignant for me. I became tearful reading it, feeling the depth of my love for David and the hope that our marriage would continue, despite the transition, then underway. Statement #12, "We are open to change," had carried us through many new experiences. Soon we would see just how far it could take us.

Another line from our vision came to mind as I wrote of our sexual struggles: "We create win-win solutions." We love this concept and attempt to fulfill it continuously, as with all the others. But it's been incredibly challenging for us to meet this one in the bedroom. My asking for what I want and David's resulting frustration and fear have led to much misunderstanding and pain. How better to quell sexual desire? Even discussing this has been challenging, as there's such disparity in our backgrounds.

I grew up in a family where we talked about everything. My mother was enthusiastic and verbal about sex, something I've always considered a gift. Despite Mom's wheelchair confinement, my parents were openly affectionate, frequently kissing and touching in the presence of us kids. They were also demonstrative with us, though my father's physical expression sometimes extended to using his belt on his offspring. Suffice it to say that there was a great deal of noise and passion in my family-of-origin, and lots of laughter, too.

David's family, on the other hand, discussed almost nothing. His parents seemed rarely to touch each other, let alone their three children. He's told me there was almost no connection among family members as he grew up. Each had done his or her own thing, oblivious to what the others were doing. Add to this mix his shame and self-contempt, magnified in the sexual realm by the irresistible, yet disgraceful, connection between his sexual pleasure and wanting to be Deborah.

David had been programmed to avoid discussion of anything of substance. His learned behavior was to shut down his thoughts and emotions, turn his back, and withdraw from anything controversial or disturbing. In contrast, I'm compelled to clear the air, attempting to understand myself and my spouse. I must share my feelings and encourage my partner's expression. Our histories were clearly ideal for creating conflict, as I pursued and he withdrew.

Relationships can be difficult—that's a given. This second marriage of ours, with its large, combined gang of kids and transgender issues, has sometimes been daunting. Even our stages of life when we wed, my children in their late teens and his youngest only four, might have created a roadblock. But remember: We'd been smitten and had gone through hell to be together. We had recognized the potential for a remarkable marriage and believed in "Us" enough to stick it out through thick and thin.

We've worked especially hard at being true to our first vision statement: "We are totally honest with each other." Since we view withholding a truth as being dishonest, this one is particularly painful and tough to honor. The combination of David's inclination to overlook troubling issues and my volatile anger caused much turbulence when things went wrong. I'd insist on discussing and resolving things, and it invariably took him more time to be open to discussion. This often had me exploding, which frightened him and caused him to clam-up.

Another huge source of pain for me was what I've called my mate's tunnel vision, a propensity to focus on just one thing, to the exclusion of all else. This trait may be desirable in a surgeon, but his disregard for my presence when we were with his children was a particular source of hurt and loneliness for me in our early years.

Undoubtedly, my spouse could add a list of ways in which living with me has been no bed of roses. But we've continued to grow and improve in our ability to remain loving, supportive, and accepting, respecting each other's differences. When we've had a challenge, we've worked through it, obtaining outside support whenever needed. In fact, I doubt we could have survived as a couple without *lots* of assistance, including several workshops using the Harville Hendrix Imago work; multiple seminars with Joyce and Barry Vissell of the Shared Heart Foundation; many Insight and personal growth workshops; and intermittent couple's therapy—including work with a specialist in stepfamily challenges. (It sure helps that all our kids are now grown!)

David and I also participated in multiple workshops and groups led by Niela, our friend and guide, at whose home we had met. We occasionally joined with other couples who were also dealing with cross-dressing issues. These gatherings were incredible opportunities for sharing and encouragement, relieving the feelings of isolation in handling this uncommon matter.

Historically, early groups for male-to-female Ts tended to focus on the physical expression of femininity, e.g., how to dress, walk, and sound like women, while neglecting the psychological aspects at play. Spouses aware of their husbands' transgenderism were virtually ignored, as if their issues did not exist or were irrelevant. With Niela's guidance, couples were encouraged to explore the ramifications of being in a transgender relationship— below the surface, as well as above. We'd found it immensely helpful to hear how other couples coped with sexual issues, matters of confidentiality, family challenges, and the like. We also appreciated sharing and discussing our own solutions and coping mechanisms.

For several years in the 80s and 90s, David—as Deborah— and I were Niela's token healthy-transgender-couple. We joined her numerous times on panels, presenting to care-givers at various clinics and hospitals, and enjoyed these experiences immensely. They provided an opportunity to educate, something which both of us value; and a good deal of personal healing and growth resulted. A bonus for David was the chance to be dressed as Deborah in public, an opportunity always eagerly seized.

I once had the most surprising question directed to me when we were on a panel at a VA hospital. There were at least thirty psychiatrists and therapists in attendance and, as usual, they'd been given the opportunity to ask questions, following our presentation. A woman in the audience asked me, "Have you ever wished you were a man?"

This seemed an odd query to me, as we were there to speak of Deborah's existence and my willingness to support the unusual proclivity in our marriage—but there it was. I was tickled by the question. I've always loved being female and the thought of being a man had never really occurred to me. After a moment's hesitation, my sense of humor kicked-in and I replied, "The only time I ever wish I were a man is on long road trips in the country, when I need a bathroom!"

Apparently, this group took the question far more seriously than I and had expected a serious answer. No one even chuckled. So much for making jokes with that humorless group!

This scenario hints at one thing essential to our unusual arrangement: A sense of humor. Years before, this attribute had been high on my list when I'd sought the ideal mate. We both place a high value on humor in this crazy world of ours, and we're delighted to make each other laugh. It's even in our relationship vision, fourth on the list: "We make time to laugh and play."

Considering the enormity of the changes in our lives, I am profoundly grateful for the solid foundation that David and I created, even before our marriage. Continually recalling and reinforcing our vision for these past two decades has held us together and will keep us together, if this is to be our fate. That and lots of laughter.

When the heart is flooded with love there is no room in it for fear,
for doubt, for hesitation. And it is this lack of fear
that makes for the dance. –Anne Morrow Lindbergh

∞

CHAPTER EIGHT
FOR GOD'S SAKE, PUT ON A DRESS!

JOURNAL ENTRY: I'm more and more aware of my ability to make choices in my life. I think that knowing I can always choose is one of my greatest lessons so far. I notice that when the old messages arise, I can almost hear Dad barking at me. Then I realize I'm free to make a different choice. This is so freeing!

Right now, I choose to be thankful. I have an incredible husband who provides the most amazing strength, support, wisdom, and love, regardless of what's happening in our lives!

∞

BY NOW YOU'RE UNDOUBTEDLY WONDERING, "What's made this woman stay in such an odd lifestyle with so strange a person?" I reiterate: Being with David has been a conscious, repetitive choice all along. I've had excellent, clear-cut reasons for wanting this man in my life for over twenty years, and one of these emerged early-on.

In 1990, shortly after we had moved into our new house, we began to make our wedding plans. In the midst of this joyful endeavor, I'd had a melt-down. I'd hit a wall of abject terror, realizing the challenges that undeniably lay ahead. Surprisingly, the cross-dressing was not my primary concern; I'd accepted that and was incorporating it into my life. My greatest fear was a more common one: Fear of the unknown that lay ahead.

With two frustrating ex-spouses, children on both sides, large amounts of alimony and child support—all on top of the transgenderism—we faced some formidable issues in a life together. For the first time (hardly the last) I asked myself, "Am I out of my mind? Am I really going to marry a guy whose ex-wife neither speaks to me nor acknowledges my existence? A man who wears dresses and has four kids, aged fourteen to three?"

My children were eighteen and fifteen—one in college, the other a thousand miles away with his dad. Why would I want to inject such chaos into my life, when it was finally becoming one of quiet reflection, self-satisfaction, and contentment? Then I realized that my greatest fear was not of the practical concerns. I'd become terrified that I might someday stop caring for David.

∞

I had once felt tremendous love for my first husband. So, as I'd begun to recognize that our marriage was no longer working, it was devastating to think of leaving the man I'd intended to be with forever. He was my children's father and we'd been crazy about each other.

We'd met right after high school and were instantly infatuated. Following an idyllic summer romance, he'd left for college in New York State and I had gone south to the University of Miami. Filled with the lust and irrationality of teenagers, we had soon found that we couldn't stand the separation. In 1969— just into our twenties and still in college—he and I were married, believing that it was for life. Twelve years later, I'd reneged on that promise.

Our first decade had been great, but the relationship began to fall apart during our eleventh year. I'd matured in those first ten years, wanting more from life than the youthful, superficial relationship that we had. Sadly, my husband seemed to remain much the same, increasing in his affinity for scotch and turning his back on me and the amazing children we'd produced. Each time I expressed dissatisfaction and a desire to resolve things, he'd say, "I'm happy with things the way they are. If you have a problem, you fix it."

By the time we landed in Massachusetts in 1979, we had up-rooted our family and moved twelve times, in six different states, ostensibly for the sake of my husband's career. Our kids were just seven and four. I'm sure we appeared the ideal American family, with a beautiful home and an abundance of creature comforts. But I'd begun to see that he and I had very different values. He was satisfied as long as he earned plenty of money and we looked good. Our marriage was crumbling and, as I began to speak of ending it, he'd told me, "You're destroying the image I've worked so hard to create."

This absurd statement and the shallow philosophy behind it had moved me closer to divorce. Sure, I liked that we made a nice-looking package, and I certainly enjoyed the material things that he provided. But our marriage had meant far more to me than its outer image. Was that really his greatest concern? By 1980, it seemed as though we were on different planes of existence, yet I was unable to convince him that a professional might help us get back on track.

Though I hadn't known it at the time, it was evidently alcoholism that prohibited my first husband from taking any responsibility for our demise. Escaping into the scotch bottle was easier for him than facing our troubles. Years later, as I learned more about the disease, I'd realized that our repeated moves were due to something known as "The Geographic Cure." This is an alcoholic behavior aimed at providing the abuser with a fresh start in a new location, whenever things go wrong. Naturally, as long as the drinking continues, the problems that existed in one place soon resurface in the next. Sure enough, my husband's job difficulties, a by-product of his excessive drinking and unresolved personal issues, showed-up in each new spot.

Just prior to the move to Massachusetts, I'd had my thirtieth birthday. Entering my fourth decade had borne with it an unusual sense of crossing an unseen threshold. There'd been no way to name or define it, though I'd tried to explain it to my mate. I just seemed to know, intuitively, that there was more to life on the other side of this mystical entryway. The experience was steering me in an exciting new direction and I knew I'd pursue it, though unaware of exactly what it was. In retrospect, I recognized the beginning of a spiritual path which became more and more conscious and compelling as I went along.

Ready for a different life, I wanted more from marriage than seemed possible with this man. If I was going to be married, I wanted true intimacy with my husband. This man's alcoholism and inability to see how his behavior was affecting our lives prohibited this. Two years after arriving in New England, I ended our marriage and entered a new domain, that of the single mom. Of necessity, I began building a tolerance for ambiguity, a skill which has served me well.

∞

Nearly a decade later, at age forty-one and planning my wedding to David, I had no desire to endure—or inflict—the pain of another divorce. My pre-wedding meltdown had rendered me a blubbering mess. Between great sobs, I'd managed to tell him, "I really loved my ex and I meant to stay with him forever. I promised I'd always love him—but I didn't. What if that happens to us?"

In David's reply, I had found immediate affirmation that he was the man for me, realizing that this relationship might actually last a lifetime. He'd taken me in his arms and gently, playfully, calmed my fears. "Don't worry about it," he'd said. "If that happens with us, at least we'll have had ten great years together!"

Such irony, this. David's assurance that a really good decade together would be better than none at all convinced me that I wanted to try for the long-haul with him. I marveled at his wisdom, insight, and tenderness, realizing that this man had the wherewithal to focus on what we *would* have together, rather than on what *might* occur. Here was the partner who'd not only created a relationship vision with me, but who would do whatever it took to honor and live that vision. I began to trust that ours would be a lasting marriage.

For our wedding in 1991, we created our own vows, promising to love each other "as long as we both are able." We had vowed in our first marriages to remain together "until death do us part." This time we were more realistic in our commitment.

As a couple's therapist with much exposure to relationships that *don't* work, I can guarantee that we've got something unusually good. In my forties, after years of experiencing the healing and transformative power of my own therapy and Insight work, I had obtained my Master's Degree in Social Work. I'd wanted to assist others in their growth and healing. A few years later, experiencing the fulfillment of a healthy relationship with David, I had extended my training, enabling me to work with couples. I sought to assist people in discovering the fulfillment of relationships in which two people are committed to their own and each other's healing, growth, and happiness.

David and I have consistently aimed at making our marriage great. Even so, as I write this, I know that some women would be long-gone by now, even those who might have accepted cross-dressing in the beginning. I still don't know what lies ahead for us and I may not know for a long time. But I know what's keeping me here now:

We have a mature acceptance of one another and the wherewithal to recognize our individual lives. This has been a guiding light in this union, each of us knowing where we end and the other begins. We're individuals.

We share a deep intimacy. While many folks automatically think of sex when this is mentioned, this is not the component to which I refer. We've found that intimacy takes many forms. Despite our struggles in the sexual realm—each of us wanting something quite different—I still pinpoint intimacy as a fundamental of our marriage.

We are innately connected through our caring, understanding, and respect for one another. Anyone who has found the proverbial soul mate knows what I mean. Those who have worked hard for decades to stay in love, maintaining respect and support, enduring multiple trials, and growing in their relationships, as we have, will appreciate what that long-term dedication stands for and why we'd want to continue it. After twenty-plus years of conscious relationship, I am still awed by the love that we have for each other.

From the beginning it was clear that we had something unique, something that others witnessed in our relationship. As part of our wedding ceremony, guests were invited to share their thoughts aloud, as a way of blessing our marriage. We were amazed by the responses, especially one from a very dear friend who stood and said that there is a "magicalness" about us. Her tears of love and happiness then rendered her speechless. The magicalness has continued and has held us together through the most difficult times.

Discussing the transgenderism with close friends through the years, I had often sensed that there was an unspoken thought, eventually voiced by one of them. The details of our conversation elude me. I was probably whining about some aspect of being married to a transgender man. She told me, "You know, Leslie, I don't think I could do what you're doing."

The simple fact is, I can't imagine *not* loving this person. I'd thought, *Why would I reject so incredible a being and the joy and fulfillment of our relationship, simply because of his need to express differently?*

I imagine for a moment that we're in a world where no one judges others. If we could simply be who we are, without all the rules and opinions, I might never question remaining with my mate, regardless of what lies ahead. This is magical thinking, of course, imagining that everyone can "live and let live." The likelihood of that happening in my lifetime seems slim, but it's a beautiful dream. In today's world, people may tell me, "But you *do* have to deal with what others think of you. You *will* be judged for being in that marriage."

Well, so be it. I look to the wisdom of Don Miguel Ruiz to guide me. In *The Four Agreements* he advises, *Don't take anything personally. ...What others say and do is a projection of their own reality. ...When you are immune to the opinions and actions of others, you won't be the victim of needless suffering.*

In our early years together, even David questioned my willingness to accept him and his proclivity. He'd occasionally ask, "How can you put up with this? I keep thinking I'll wake up one day and you'll have asked yourself, 'What am I doing with you?' and you'll be gone."

My first response was to remind him to watch his self-fulfilling prophecies. Then I'd assure him that everything I loved about him, and how he loved me, far outweighed any challenges to my accepting his transgenderism. Sometimes I'd just get annoyed. It seemed he doubted my ability to judge character and determine what I wanted in a mate. I'd reiterate that I was accustomed to having the best; that it was insulting to me that he'd suggest I'd settle for anything less!

Undoubtedly, his fears of my leaving stemmed from lifelong self-judgment and loathing for the transgender part of himself. His negative judgments about cross-dressing seemed to obliterate any awareness of how remarkable an individual he was. It appeared that he was oblivious to the reality of the many others who loved and admired him, and of all the reasons he *was* lovable and admirable.

Another reply to my doubtful partner was to point out the contrast to what has occurred in my family. After all, everything is relative. I'd had two siblings who killed themselves. When David spoke of his desire and need to put on women's clothes, I was filled with wonder at the innocuous simplicity of cross-dressing as the antidote to his angst. "Big deal," I'd tell him. "Remember what's happened in my family when people were unhappy? If it makes you happy to put on a dress, for God's sake, put on a dress!"

I've always felt honored to be able to encourage my spouse to follow his bliss. It's rarely diminished my own happiness—and he has done the same for me. This mutuality has led us to wonder about a phenomenon I've dubbed "The Gift of the Magi" syndrome.

The story, by O. Henry, tells of a young, 19th century couple, very much in love, each of whom has a treasured possession. The wife's long, luxuriant hair is her crowning glory and she longs for the beautiful set of combs she's spied in a shop window. Her husband's treasure is the gold watch his father and grandfather owned before him, though he lacks a fob chain to hold it in place.

As Christmas nears, the wife spies a beautiful watch chain in a store window and sells her abundant hair for the cash to purchase it. Meanwhile her husband, knowing how his wife has admired those combs, hocks his watch to purchase them for her. Upon presentation of the gifts, each is astonished to discover that the other has given up the object that he or she most treasures, to bestow a precious gift on the loved one.

Knowing this story and its message, I've playfully borrowed its name to identify what my spouse and I do with each other. We've occasionally found ourselves bending over backward to make certain that the other is happy and satisfied, sometimes negating our own first choice. Calling this degree of caring "The Gift of the Magi Syndrome" has provided us much kidding and laughter through the years.

Years ago, when the country was abuzz with the concept of codependency, we became concerned about giving things up for the other. In our desire to be psychologically healthy, we began to explore what that meant. According to the concept of codependency, it seemed that nearly every act of kindness in a relationship, any little sacrifice for the other, was a sign of a disorder, demonstrating unhealthy boundaries, neediness, unworthiness, self-denial.

Ultimately, we realized that the choices each of us makes to provide for the other are just that, choices. Being conscious of them, while each of us continues our self-care, and discussing issues that arise: This is how we *choose* to be in our marriage.

Early in our relationship, David had an awareness that brought relief to both of us. A pattern had developed after we moved in together. Whenever he mentioned the desire to dress, I'd begin calling friends and making dinner or weekend plans to ensure his cross-dressing opportunities. Eventually, I realized that I'd become the queen bee of arrangements for our cross-dressing social life, and recognized the *true* codependency of my actions. I had eventually grown tired of it and told him he could start making his own plans to be Deborah.

After we'd delved into this and discussed it ad nauseum, David realized that sometimes it was just *telling* me of his desire to put on women's clothing that he needed. Since there'd never been anyone he could talk to about it before therapy with Niela, being able to share his reviled need with me brought him comfort and a sense of well-being; nothing further was needed. This relieved my sense of urgency to create cross-dressing opportunities, and we had both learned from the experience.

Lest you mistakenly believe that we have never stooped to bickering or juvenile displays of egotism and selfishness, let me assure you that we are human and we've argued plenty. Like every couple, we have disagreements, major and minor. We can be as self-centered and immature, as belligerent, as the next couple! However, we've remained committed to resolving whatever comes up, resuming as quickly as possible the loving-kindness that we want to express in our marriage and in the world. Our desire to nurture and maintain our conscious relationship brings us back to humility and forgiveness, and we work hard at letting go of the negativity—once our sanity returns.

A prized relic of the Insight Seminars remains with us, providing perfect guidance for our lives: *Use everything for your learning, upliftment, and growth.* I can think of no better way to deal with whatever shows up in life. Perhaps, somehow, I'd known this intuitively from a very early age.

The part of you that loves you more than anything else has created roadblocks to lead you to yourself. Without something pricking you in the side saying, 'Look here! This way!' you are not going to go in the right directions. –A. H. Almaas

∾

CHAPTER NINE
ROADBLOCKS TO MYSELF

JOURNAL ENTRY: God, what a horrendous week. I've been short-tempered, critical, a real bitch. I did a Psychodrama training last weekend and was flooded with old rage and hurt, then spent the week dumping all the bullshit on the one closest to me. I couldn't stand the way I was treating David—it was so unfair. But at the same time, I felt helpless to stop. Thank God for this awareness. It helped settle me and my feelings a bit. I continue to be amazed at these age-old emotions. Don't they ever get all cleaned out?

∾

FOR YEARS, PEOPLE HAVE WONDERED at my ability to be in a transgender marriage. This—and my own need for clarity—have led me to examine my first six decades, attempting to name the sources of my willingness to live with differences. True, not everyone dealing with similar life circumstances would have gone in the directions I've chosen; but an innate optimism enables me to trust in the goodness of outcomes.

For starters, as my mother observed and recorded in my baby book, I began life happily. This joyful essence has been nearly constant through all of my life and I'm immensely grateful for it. I've also developed the capacity to view all things that have come my way as learning tools. (Generally, in retrospect, I'm sorry to add; only rarely in the midst of them!) And I have long recognized the blessings of tenacity and resiliency in my life.

The story of my mother's paralysis and its impact provide the earliest signs of my capacity for adjusting to diversity. I grew up in a family that was physically different, attracting attention wherever we went: A woman in a wheelchair, pushed full-speed ahead by my athletic father, surrounded by four scurrying kids, like a gaggle of geese and goslings.

I was three when polio struck my mom in 1952. My brothers were seven and two; my sister, five. We were Baby Boomers, the four of us born in just five years—products of the post-WWII trend to reproduce somewhat like rabbits.

My father Jack was a dashing 1944 Naval Academy graduate who'd been a pilot in the war. Mother Edi, busy reproducing, nursing an infant, and chasing toddlers, somehow also found time for tennis and bridge. Her household activities extended to painting the entire house. I'm told she was a fireball on her feet. There's an iconic, 1940-something photo of my mother in Hawaii, halfway up a palm tree, with a coconut—in its hull—clenched in her teeth.

My mother's illness, a year before the Salk vaccine was developed, brought devastation and tremendous change to our family. Mom lay in an iron lung in Virginia for six weeks, her survival uncertain. There was great concern that we kids would contract polio as well. I'm sure that fear was palpable in the household as my father frantically arranged care for us, his beloved Edi languishing near death.

Explanations to us children would have been minimal; parents of the 1950s were not inclined to discuss things with their kids. In any case, our tender ages negated much understanding. To keep us safe and cared-for, we three younger ones were sent to live with relatives in other states. My father, glued to mom's side for weeks, kept my older brother with him, as he was the only one in school. My sister and I went to Florida; our little brother was taken, alone, to New York State by our maternal grandparents.

I have no memory of my mother's illness or of being sent away, nor do I recall a walking mother. I have harbored a sense that I was somehow under my older sister's wing, despite our being just three- and five-years-old. It seems significant to my well-being that I went with a sibling, rather than by myself. My sister and I, undoubtedly traumatized by the terrifying separation from mother and home, were cared-for by a childless great aunt and uncle.

One result of this early separation has been the challenge of sporadic abandonment issues—of feeling terrifyingly alone in the world. Blessedly, with the help of some wonderful clinicians, healing workshops, and a spouse who's been a solid, trustworthy anchor, I've recovered from the most devastating feelings of being adrift on my own.

Nearly a year passed before our family of six reassembled in Virginia, with Mom confined to a wheelchair, disabled and physically weak. It must have been obvious that my father could not remain in the Navy, as leaving a paraplegic wife and four young kids for long cruises was out of the question. Dad resigned, ending the naval career he'd always desired, and the family moved to his hometown Tampa.

It was years before I realized the unusual nature of my parents' relationship, of Jack's exceptional devotion to Edi. My first real inkling occurred one day in my teen years, when I complained about my dad's disciplinary methods to the great aunt who'd cared for me a decade before. She had chastised me, saying that I must never say anything negative about my father. "Listen here," she lectured. "Most men in your father's situation would have left your mother long ago. Don't you ever let me hear you speak that way again about that wonderful man!"

This had been the first indication that my father's behavior was, apparently, above reproach. As I grew, I was aware of his gargantuan efforts to care for Mom, though my understanding was filtered through typical adolescent narcissism. My father's devotion to his wife extended to all manner of loving care for forty-five years after the polio. Until back problems began in his forties, he lifted her in and out of the car, bed, airplane seats, on and off our sailboat—even at low tide, when there was a four foot drop from dock to boat! He gave her bedpans, carrying that cold metal device in its own little suitcase when they went on trips.

Dad took my mother almost everywhere they wanted to go. One sweet memory is of family outings to the beach, when he'd carry her from the car to a lounge chair he'd set-up near the water's edge. Later, he would sweep her up again and head into the Gulf, plopping her—butt first—into an inner tube, with us kids holding it steady. As we four bobbed around Mom and Dad in the salty waves, it had seemed as though we were actually a normal, healthy family.

My parents' roles were reversed in later years, when my father began showing signs of Alzheimer's disease in his mid-sixties. Despite Mom's infirmity and the growing weakness of post-polio syndrome, her kindness and patience with Dad's gradual decline seemed unlimited. Once, when visiting them as an adult, I heard my mother request that Dad put her shoes on her, something he'd done for decades before. Next, I heard the coaching required to help him complete the task. "No, Darling, that's a lamp," Mom said, following her initial request. "No, Jack, that's a book; yes, those are my shoes. No, Darling, that's the wrong foot. Yes, that's the one."

I'd asked her how she could do it; how she could remain so loving and tolerant, repeating the simple instructions, never losing her temper or patience. Her reply was intense, almost angry: "This man has cared for me for fifty years, Leslie. Do you think I could turn my back on him now, just because he has trouble understanding?"

Mother's criteria for moving Dad to a nursing home were incontinence and an inability to recognize her. Finally, after ten years, the criteria were met. Dad lived for three more years away from home, dying suddenly of a heart attack at the age of seventy-nine.

My parents lived a profound love story. It was an exceptional model of caring, accepting, and adjusting, despite all challenges that arose in their lives. Observing this relationship model for forty years paved the way for me to love David, despite his unusual proclivity. As with my parents' illnesses, he'd certainly not chosen to be transgender.

Respite from the chaos of the Hilburn household had come in the form of childhood summers in Pennsylvania, at the vacation home of my Florida great aunt and uncle. In winter, they lived down the street from us in Tampa. Summers, they headed to the mountains. They were like grandparents to us kids and had taken two of us north to their farm each summer. Wealthy and generous, they'd become the fairy godparents of the entire family, taking their siblings, nieces, and nephews on trips and shopping excursions. They bought us extravagant gifts and opened both homes to much extended family.

Summers were full of excitement: Riding horses, hiking, sailing, and lots of joyful gatherings. Northern family members congregated at the Pennsylvania farm on weekends and special occasions, for picnics, swimming, games, and overnights. My maternal grandparents were just two hours away in New York State, so we saw them often, too.

It was an adventure to be away from our own folks for the entire season. I was able to observe and learn much from the comings and goings of different sets of relatives, just as a kid at summer camp is exposed to new ideas and ways of seeing the world. There were rich opportunities to expand my awareness of who I wanted to be as an adult—and who I did *not* want to become.

I was exposed to radically different religious views during those summers. My great aunt and grandmother, her sister, were High Episcopalians. They were determined to influence us Hilburn kids in the religious realm, since our parents had fled more traditional faith for the liberalism of the Unitarian church. I still vividly recall my grandmother snorting with contempt, "Hmph—Unitarians! They're the ones who give God the summer off!"

Throughout each season, we were taken to Episcopal churches in Pennsylvania and New York, contrasting vividly with our Unitarian experience. I readily discerned the disparate philosophies and practices of the two religions, and this had led me to begin formulating my own spiritual choices.

My aunt's and uncle's wealth and privilege seemed to garner a certain degree of haughtiness that I found distasteful. So, I learned much about differences, even among families; about principles that varied. There were certain forms of entitlement that I observed, eventually moving me in the direction of compassion and a desire to understand others who differed from me.

My parents seemed far more open-minded and compassionate toward folks who were unlike them. Through close exposure to both viewpoints, I began to devise my own philosophy of life. It was much like having two separate childhoods: The more open-minded, liberal scenario in my parents' home (albeit loaded with structure and discipline), interspersed with the dogmatic, yet extravagant lifestyle of my generous relatives. These idyllic childhood summers assisted me in creating a solid philosophy of tolerance, acceptance, and flexibility. Something innate seemed to guide me in choosing what worked for me and instinctively using all that I observed and experienced for my growth, development, and awareness.

Enormous adaptability was required after my first child's birth in 1972. Despite a planned pregnancy and easy experience with childbirth, I'd sunken into a severe postpartum depression within a week of my daughter's appearance. Unable to fathom a way out of it, I'd asked for help, then spent several frightening weeks hospitalized and months to recover. Beyond fearing that I'd never be happy again, I was most terrified of following in the footsteps of my paternal grandmother.

Dad's mother had suffered a post partum *psychosis*, a more serious disorder, after her third child's birth. She'd completely lost touch with reality. When this occurred and she was institutionalized, it was 1926—a time when no pharmaceutical aid and little real help existed for treatment of the mentally ill. Eventually diagnosed with paranoid schizophrenia, she endured a lifetime of repetitive hospitalizations. My siblings and I accepted this reality about our grandmother, though we lacked explanations or any real clarity regarding her mental illness. We simply loved a grandma who made the best fudge in the world, and she loved us right back.

Between breakdowns and treatment, our grandmother was a wonderfully sane, kind, and loving woman. She was brilliant; an artist who had taught school and spoke Spanish as well as her native English. At times she was completely lucid for months, so much so that my parents had her stay with us when they spent an infrequent weekend away from home.

My father had become his mother's guardian in his thirties, when his own father died suddenly. For years, Dad had to commit his mother for treatment, whenever the inevitable dark cloud would descend and she'd become unsafe to herself. My grandmother would hear voices from pictures on the wall, or from a radio or TV that wasn't turned-on. Once she'd nearly had her feet amputated, having followed the commands of these voices. For weeks, she'd been soaking her feet in vegetable oil, then encasing her oiled lower legs in support hose. This odd routine caused the decomposition of the skin on her feet and ankles. Fortunately, my father discovered the bizarre behavior in time and her feet were saved, but it was clear that grandma needed hospitalizing again.

We kids, children of a paraplegic mother, were often called-upon to assist with things Mom couldn't handle. For one particular task, an adult would have been more suitable, though my proximity must have made me the logical choice for this one. I was about eleven or twelve when Dad said he needed me to come along as he took my grandmother to Tampa General Hospital. I'd been horrified by the reply when I asked, "Why do you need me to go with you?"

I think it was Mom who told me, "Daddy needs you to keep your grandma from jumping out of the car on the way to the hospital."

I was shocked to think that my dad would do this to his own mother against her will, let alone that she might try to jump from our moving car—and that I was to prevent this! I sat in the passenger seat while dad drove, my dear grandmother between us. We'd traveled without incident, then left her in a locked ward. In my young mind, we had betrayed her.

I'd learned early that my family was different. But that didn't stop us from handling things as they came, whatever that meant, and continuing to love and care for each other, a fact that still amazes me. Considering some of the obstacles my parents faced, it seems remarkable that we appeared as normal as we did; but wasn't that the expectation of the fifties and early sixties?

In the early seventies, on Valentine's Day, I became a suicide survivor. (That's anyone close to someone who kills

4444444444

himself.) I'd been out of the hospital for only three months, continuing my struggle with postpartum depression, learning to be a mom to my seven-month-old daughter. With my fighting spirit, I'd determined that I would stay alive and find my way back to the joy I'd experienced throughout my young life; to the happiness Mom had written about in my baby book.

When the doorbell rang that February day, my mother-in-law stood on my doorstep, with a close friend of hers beside her. This was odd. My husband's mother was not someone to stop by unannounced, and I couldn't imagine why she'd appeared with a friend. I can only guess how they thought this visit might go, needing a team of two to deliver the news.

I ushered them in and was quickly told that my younger brother had shot himself. I'd thought this strange; we were not a family of gun-carriers. I had innocently pictured my brother shooting himself in the foot, accidently, though it was soon clear how inaccurate a thought this was.

He had intentionally shot himself in the head, in his old bedroom, as Mom made a pancake breakfast at the other end of the house. The image I've never been able to shake is of my mother, wheeling herself to his bedroom, hoping against hope that what she'd heard had not been a gunshot.

By the time I was told, my younger brother was brain-dead and on life support, soon to be discontinued. I'd had no forewarning of this horrific event, though I later learned that my parents had been vividly aware of their youngest child's slide into psychosis. Having graduated from college the previous spring, he'd been struggling with depression and direction in his life, so he'd moved back into our parents' home for support. He'd begun to express paranoia about unusual things, such as a helicopter passing overhead. Complicating his troubles was a break-up with a girlfriend, who'd then moved away. Evidently, his depression was deeper, the illness more grave, than anyone had realized.

Questions will always remain: How do others know when more help is needed? Who will endure psychosis; who will choose death instead? What compels some individuals to end the assault of mental illness in this final, horrific manner? As I've imagined my parents' efforts to handle what was occurring in

50

their son's life, I know that no reliable answers exist. Those of us who've dealt with suicide are left with only unanswered questions and devastation.

Just a few months before my sibling's death, I'd been petrified of my own depression and feelings of inadequacy as a mother. I was convinced that *anyone* was more capable of caring for my infant than I. Yet, despite briefly thinking that death might be the only way out of my pain, I never lost sight of two deep convictions: That killing myself would be completely unfair to others, an infliction on my husband and family; and that I'd once been a happy person who'd loved life. I'd known that there *had* to be a way to get back there.

I never became psychotic, or out of touch with reality; yet, I was still powerless to resume my once-joyful life. Fortunately, something within compelled me to ask for help when I couldn't go on; to accept that help, though terrified by the idea and experience of hospitalization, and the fear of repeating my grandmother's disordered life. Logic, if nothing else, had forced me to find a way to survive, but my brother had been incapable of these life-saving thoughts.

As with other life events, I've managed to use the horrific loss of my brother to gain more perspective on life. Most things pale by comparison to suicide. It's part of what allowed me, many years later, to accept David's choices to dress and, ultimately, transition. As I'd told him, "You know what happens in my family when people are unhappy."

Another life-changing incident was my sister's coming-out as a lesbian in 1977. This was an opportunity to shift my perspective away from the straight and narrow, opening my mind and heart along the way.

We'd had a double wedding in 1969, a unique choice that was practical, too, since our older brother was also marrying that summer. About six years into our marriages, my sister and her husband were coming unraveled. She had visited us, revealing that she'd become attracted to one of their women friends. I admit, I was shocked. Growing up in the fifties and sixties, surrounded by and infused with homophobia, this was not something I'd ever considered a possibility among my siblings. It just never occurred to me.

I recall my reaction, surprising to me now, but it's a reflection of my naiveté at the time. I thought I was open-minded then, yet there were clearly limits to my ability to accept. When she'd mentioned lesbianism, I remember saying something like, "Oh, no, Sis! You don't have to *be* one of those! Can't you just have them as your friends?" (Even using the word "lesbian" felt taboo to me then.)

During my sister's stay, she'd gradually familiarized me with the concept of women loving women. It was fairly new to her, too, I suppose; but she managed to pave the way for me to accept her dawning recognition of a different sexual orientation. As a seasoned psychotherapist, she had gently turned my objections and concerns back into questions to me. Neither defensive nor angry, she never tried to cram anything down my throat; she simply kept drawing me back to answering my questions for myself.

It was about six months later that we saw each other again. She was living in New Orleans, and I mentioned that I'd love to visit her during Mardi Gras. Her simple reply was her coming-out to me: "Sure," she'd said, "as long as you don't mind hanging-out with my lesbian friends."

By then, I was only mildly surprised. For months, I'd pondered her undemanding explanation of what it means to be a lesbian. Just to make sure of what she was implying, I'd quietly asked, "So, does that mean that you're one, too?"

"Yep," was her easy reply, and she'd beamed at me, clearly at ease with her new identity.

I'd known immediately that I was prepared to accept her new lifestyle, and this had been my first conscious experience of loving unconditionally. I'd realized that I loved my sister without reserve; that I always would, *regardless*. True, I wasn't crazy about her new lifestyle, but that's because I'm heterosexual. I couldn't quite grasp why she'd want a woman lover, but what difference did that make? It would have no bearing on my life, and I could see absolutely no reason why it might destroy our relationship or diminish my love for her.

∞

My version of "having it all" in the eighties? It was divorce, single motherhood, and raising my two children alone. I had an occasional date, some fun with women friends, many financial struggles. College, working, a business of my own; and my most important task, raising my kids, both challenged and gratified me. I grew and healed, finding a plethora of ways to thrive, and generally loved my life.

At thirty-five, I graduated from college, magna cum laude. I studied A Course in Miracles, a self-taught program focusing on forgiveness and peace of mind. I opened to greater spiritual awareness and discovery. I did the Insight Seminars and therapy, working hard to heal all the old wounds. And I grew in self-esteem and connection to others. I exercised, did yoga and gradually recovered from my brother's death.

I was a member, then president, of our local chapter of the National Organization for Women. I traveled with my kids, taking them to visit friends and relatives, and to a favorite conference center in Rowe, MA, where we all opened our minds and hearts. I joined the monthly gatherings with the Women's Floating Circle and felt like a free spirit, looking for new ways to dance through my life, prepared for new experiences.

In the midst of my broadening horizons, of raising my kids, loving my life, and exploring new possibilities, I was slammed with the news of my sister's suicide. I'd not known, at that time, that the likelihood of additional suicides increases in families where one has already occurred. Independence Day, 1987 must have signified an odd kind of freedom for my sister. Freedom from her tortured mind? I can only guess.

She lived in California by then and loved it, though our living on opposite coasts made for infrequent get-togethers. Nine months earlier, we'd met in New York, to visit our grandmother there. I'd seen that my sister was quite depressed. She'd allowed me to comfort her in her distress and I'd felt oddly privileged by this. After all, she was the psychotherapist; it would be a decade before I joined the profession.

Until that time, she had always been the strong, wise, older sister—my support. She invariably had all the right answers, teaching me about our family dynamics and how to deal with the resulting damage. She'd been a spiritual guide, too, providing me with new ideas, books, and courses to pursue. Like all of our family members, my sister was a suicide survivor. She, too, had experienced the devastation of our brother's violent death. The thought of her taking that same route had never entered my mind, and I'd had no inkling of the difficulty and depth of her struggle.

Oddly, that Fourth of July was a strange day for me. Twice, I had spontaneously burst into unprovoked tears. I'd chalked it up to being alone, away from extended family, and recalling the joy-filled summer celebrations of my youth. By evening, I was reveling in a rare day to myself, having sent my kids off with friends to a town fair. But my peace was shattered when the phone rang and my sister's friend began to speak. It had felt unreal. As if I were in a movie or novel, she'd asked me, "Are you sitting down, Leslie? I have some terrible news."

I'd immediately flashed back to another call from this woman, seven months earlier. She had reached me on Christmas Eve, a few weeks after I'd seen my sister—so depressed—and told me that she'd been hospitalized for a manic episode. My sister had stopped keeping appointments with her psychotherapy clients, saying that she was healing them psychically. Friends had found her naked, in her apartment, her belongings piled near the door. In her disordered state, she was convinced that she no longer needed anything material to exist.

When the call came that Fourth of July, I'd guessed what was coming next. Suddenly, my earlier tears made sense; I'd had a premonition of tragedy. "Just tell me what it is," I had managed to say through clenched teeth, my heart already breaking.

"Leslie, your sister hung herself this morning. She's dead," she'd blurted. Then immediately, "I'm sorry; I'm sorry. Oh, God, Leslie, I'm so very sorry."

Despite my having quickly imagined this was the news, it still took a moment to register fully. I fought to maintain my own sanity; spoke a few words, attempting normalcy, while vainly seeking the calm I'd been feeling. Then I'd begun to crumble, the horrific reality sinking-in.

The loss of my only sister will never make sense to me. I've worked hard to let her go, though I will long for her presence in my life until I die. There are questions I wish she could answer, the first a simple, "Why didn't you call me before you did it?" I'd have done anything to save her: Gone to California immediately; stayed with her; brought her with me to Massachusetts; sat with her through whatever needed to occur—anything to keep her alive. But in the twenty-five years since her death, I've come to realize that she'd seen no other choice for ending her inner torment, just as with our brother, fourteen years before. She'd taken the only action guaranteed to end her suffering. Even with her abundant knowledge, resources, and many friends in the therapeutic world, she could not be saved.

Beyond all else, surviving my beloved sister's death has shown me how strong and sane I am. Years before, mired in depression, I had somehow possessed the capacity to ask for help and receive it. I'd been gifted, perhaps at conception, with a different brain chemistry; one that allowed me the wherewithal and clarity to remember my former life of joy; to recall the remarkable reasons for staying alive. My remaining healthy and whole, when my sister had always seemed the stronger, wiser of us, is a great irony—almost beyond belief.

On the west coast for her services, I had found it imperative to promise my parents that I'd never kill myself for any reason. As I spoke, I'd instantly realized that this pledge was more for me than for anyone else. I knew for a fact that I'd survive, striving continually to make my life more worthwhile, more beautiful, more joyful.

Dragging myself through the next five months, leaning on others and tending my gaping wound, I mechanically prepared for the next chapter of my life. Turns out, it was the Floating Circle, that following December, bringing David and Deborah to me. Something within that man in purple, determined to let Deborah have her voice, had called to the triumphant spirit in me. Whatever drew us together, whatever lay ahead, a bond was created that day at Niela's, one that unmistakably ensured an enduring allegiance to our mutual support, devotion, and love.

PART TWO
ON OUR WAY

On Lake Winnipesaukee, New Hampshire, 2009

Perhaps you worry in the night because it comes to you that
you are different. I love you because you are different....
In the end it comes to this: you are human. Yes, so am I.
And I love you for it. And I love you for yourself. –Kenneth Sawyer

∞

CHAPTER TEN
ENDOCRINOLOGY ENTERS OUR LIVES

JOURNAL ENTRY: We're staying in Boston tonight and tomorrow morning we see Dr. Safer, the endocrinologist. We've just returned from a wonderful dinner and agreed—this is a celebration. It's a major step in a journey of uncertainty and exploration, that's for sure. And I still have no idea what this will mean for us in the long run. At least there's no question of the love we're both feeling, and that's worth celebrating.

∞

FOR TWENTY YEARS, after an evening out or an event with David dressed as Deborah, I'd watch my husband resume a masculine role and observe his great frustration and pain. He'd remove the feminine trappings, then I'd hold him as he wept.

Attempting to relieve his own suffering, he'd done intermittent therapy for two decades, consuming an assortment of antidepressants. For years he'd attended Niela's support groups and experienced much personal growth through seminars and workshops. He even had the freedom to be Deborah fairly often, with my encouragement. But none of this brought lasting happiness to my mate. Hiding his femme self, returning to his masculine role, invariably brought waves of grief. We knew that this was a common experience among transgendered folks, but where was the relief in that awareness? Adding to his anguish was the paradox that, while he loved the cross-dressing, the shame persisted.

By 2008, David was so agitated much of the time that it became unpleasant for me to be with him for more than a few days. With greater free time than he had, I'd escape, alone, to our summer cabin in New Hampshire. There, I'd delight in my solitude and refill my cup, so to speak, then return to my habitually-unhappy spouse. Our marriage was solid and fulfilling, but it was better in short spurts. It had gotten to be pretty aggravating to be around him, and we both knew this was related to his mounting frustration in shutting-down Deborah's expression.

Fluctuating between encouragement and exasperation, I observed my mate's self-inflicted judgments, wondering how he could continue to do this to himself. We'd learned in Insight Seminars and espoused the philosophy that, when we don't like something, we can change either the situation or our feelings about it, nothing else. I was stymied by how this incredible being could live with the conundrum of reveling in his feminine expression, while also feeling such hatred for what he was doing. He seemed unable to alter the negative self-judgment, yet he certainly wasn't going to give up the cross-dressing.

I'm sure it was discouraging to David that I supported and encouraged his expression as Deborah, yet took pleasure in knowing those times would pass and my man would return to me. I loved him regardless, but preferred having a husband, for the long-term. David rarely put his own needs ahead of mine, wanting to ensure my happiness and maintain a gratifying relationship. We were truly that "Gift of the Magi" couple: I'd promote Deborah's expression, favoring the man of my dreams; he'd attempt to be satisfied with short doses of Deborah, then bring my husband back.

Eventually, there was no denying David's transsexuality. He began to verbalize this awareness in 2009, though he lacked the belief that some action might result. However, I'd lived with his pain for two decades. By the fall of that year, I was unwilling to watch him try one more antidepressant, hoping for relief from a near-constant malaise. As he spoke again of a new therapist, a new drug to alleviate depression, I surprised us both by suggesting an alternative, which we knew to be an elixir for the transgendered. "I just don't think it's another antidepressant you need, Sweetie," I'd said. "I think it's time to talk to an endocrinologist and investigate female hormones."

David was shocked, hardly believing my suggestion. This radical solution had never seemed a possibility to him, though we were both aware of the relief and joy experienced by transsexuals who begin consuming hormones of the opposite sex. He'd been astonished that I'd proposed it, immediately asking, "You *really* want me to do this? Are you *sure*?"

After several days of disbelief and discussion, David accepted my encouragement to pursue this course and scheduled with a Boston endocrinologist who treats many transsexuals. However, even after his appointment with Dr. Safer, he hesitated to proceed with the necessary blood work so that he could begin the medications. We lived sixty miles from Boston, so it would be logical to use our local hospital for routine procedures such as this; but this was the very hospital where he saw patients and performed surgeries. Patient confidentiality notwithstanding, he imagined word leaking-out.

The magnitude of proceeding also deterred him, as we both considered how taking these next steps would alter our lives. Ultimately, he reached the edge of the proverbial cliff—and then, he leapt. He had the tests locally, trusting that the confidentiality safeguards would hold, and began taking female hormones and testosterone blocker.

We were never sure, later, whether word leaked-out around the hospital because of the testing, or whether the news simply got around, as he'd begun revealing his plan to more and more people there. It was a titillating topic; hard to imagine people keeping it to themselves!

For the first few months on the medications, David continued to ask me, almost daily, "Are you absolutely sure you're okay with this? I'll stop immediately if going ahead means losing you."

I had told him from the start, "Look, I know you need to do this; there's no question in my mind. I don't want to watch you suffering anymore. But I can't possibly know what this will mean for us down the road, so please stop asking me to tell you."

The idea of my spouse continuing to suppress his soul's longing, in order to keep me in our marriage, seemed ludicrous to me. I imagined on-going denial on his part would eventually lead to further misery, a martyrdom, of sorts. While I appreciated David's willingness to stop the progression toward his life-long yearning, I simply wouldn't be in a marriage under those conditions. The transition was underway; my husband would begin living as a woman someday soon. And there was no question that I, too, was transitioning—an obvious necessity, under the circumstances.

If you ask me what I came into this world to do, I will tell you:
I came to live out loud. –Emile Zola

CHAPTER ELEVEN
"I'VE GOT TO TELL THEM"

JOURNAL ENTRY: The lure of being Deborah is becoming more and more intense for D. He tells me daily how hard it is to put a hold on this movement toward being her. But I still need more time for this transition, and I think D needs it too. A clear time period to make the transition, not jumping from male to female in one quick, felled swoop.

I sometimes wonder if there will come a day when we'll forget she was ever a man. Krishnamurti said, "Freedom from the desire for an answer is essential to the understanding of a problem." This reminds me of my aim to tolerate ambiguity. God, is my life ever full of it now!

IT WAS A SUNDAY in November, 2010. David had been on hormones for about a year and the need to exist full-time as Deborah seemed greater each day. We sat in a pew of the small Unitarian-Universalist Church we'd attended for five years and had come to love, feeling close to this community of like-minded folks. The service had been sweet, with the desired effect of warming our hearts and touching our souls.

As the congregation drifted downstairs for coffee hour, David turned to me, looking pained. "I can't do this any longer," he said quietly. "I can't sit here anymore with these people we love, people who love us, and not be *me*. I've got to tell them what I'm doing."

"Talk to the minister," I suggested. "John will understand, and I bet he'll have some ideas about what to do next. Please tell him what's going on."

Our beloved minister, Reverend John Pastor, is a gay man with a husband; he's familiar with the struggles and pain of being different. He had known about Deborah, had met "her" in our home, and I knew he'd provide some comfort and insight into this latest challenge. I went downstairs with the others, while the two of them remained upstairs through most of the coffee hour.

When I finally came looking for my husband, I found him in the sanctuary with John, both of them near tears. John had known that David was planning to transition and had been encouraging him through the process, emphasizing the need to be true to him(her)self. He'd had no trouble understanding David's dilemma, the growing need to reveal Deborah, versus remaining safely in the closet.

Later that day, David said that John had talked about connection as the true meaning of spirituality. He'd emphasized the importance of loving and accepting oneself first, as a requisite for fully connecting with spouse, family, friends, and others, including Spirit. He'd been pleased and touched that David had reached the cusp of revealing Deborah's existence to our church community. "Disconnection means isolation," John had told him.

He'd encouraged David to come-out to our congregation, offering the pulpit for a Sunday in January 2011, for this purpose. This suggestion was not unusual, as John is a half-time minister, and services on alternate Sundays are led by parishioners or guests. What *would* be different was an entire service centered on Deborah's coming-out. The opportunity was irresistible.

David, as Deborah, had already spoken in several churches in other New England towns, explaining the transgender phenomenon and what it meant to him, to us. The reception had invariably been positive; perhaps it would be with our congregation, as well. We could only hope that exposing this surprising dimension of our lives to our fellow parishioners would not diminish their caring and support.

Since the journey belonged to both of us, we decided to do the service together. We'd spoken before in this church, revealing some of our innermost selves, though never the secret of David's transgenderism. We would come-out together to this community.

Creating services together had been exciting for us; we enjoy the collaboration. We're comfortable as speakers, write well and are articulate, and enjoy the opportunity to entertain, inform, and, presumably, inspire. Our styles and personalities are quite different and we balance one another in our presentations. A plan for our service emerged, but not without some trepidation. David was going public with a shocking revelation in the town where he practiced medicine.

We invited a number of friends, non-members of our church, to join the congregation for our service, seeking their moral support. Despite knowing about David's transgenderism, some had never seen him in his feminine role. Here was an opportunity to present Deborah from a safe distance, while also providing an education about it.

We had some concern that this secret was simply too sensational to remain within the sanctity of our church; it would have been foolish to think otherwise. We were apprehensive that the medical staff would get wind of it and—possibly even more disquieting—Dr. Fabian's patients. Nevertheless, we both knew that it was time to proceed, regardless. We prepared to go public and readied ourselves, mentally and emotionally, for all of the city of Gardner to know.

That was the thing about the world: it wasn't that things were harder than you thought they were going to be, it was that they were hard in ways that you didn't expect. –Lev Grossman

∽

CHAPTER TWELVE
MULTI-FACETED PAIN

JOURNAL ENTRY: Okay, what's happening with me now? It's weariness with discussing the transition and all that's happening. I'm so sick of everything in our lives revolving around this change, so tired of explaining it to the folks who know that it's happening and want to know more. It's sadness at losing my husband. And it's fear at what may occur in our relationship. It continues to be a beautiful friendship with lots of affection—but it seems to be morphing away from romance and any sexual intimacy. Lots of sadness and loss going-on for me. D knows it and feels sad for me, too.

∞

THROUGH OUR YEARS TOGETHER, preparing for trips on which David might dress as Deborah meant that he'd looked to me for advice on appropriate outfits. "Should I bring along some Deborah clothes?" he'd ask. "Do you think I'll be able to dress?" Or, depending on the purpose and destination of our travels, "I don't think I'll take any of David's clothes at all. What do you think?"

I'd been fashion consultant and stylist for my transgender husband for two decades. It was a practical matter. Since most Ts lack the background and personal experience for choosing women's clothing or styling longer hair and applying make-up, they almost always need outside advice in putting themselves together as presentable females.

We'd gone to Florida for the 2010 holidays, spending most of our time in the Keys. With its diverse population, Key West is one of the places where David, in femme persona, felt safe and carefree. My spouse spent the entire four days as Deborah, loving every minute.

As we'd packed for the Christmas trip, I was suggesting what David might wear as Deborah. Much to his chagrin, there was also the need for a few guy-clothes, since we'd be visiting our Florida daughter and son-in-law in another part of the state. They'd been aware and accepting of David's cross-dressing and knew that he was now on female hormones, but we'd be attending a party with folks who knew nothing of Deborah's existence. So, along with the feminine things, I was grabbing outfits for David, matching slacks to shirts.

"Hey, Honey, how 'bout this plaid shirt I bought you in Hilton Head?" I'd asked. "You hardly ever wear it and I really love it."

The fact is, *whenever* I'd chosen male clothes for my spouse—nearly all of which I'd purchased for him—any enthusiasm was mine. For years it had pained me to see how little David cared for his masculine appearance. As we packed, I had mistakenly (unrealistically?) thought he might be happy to dress to please me, for what little time he remained a man. Was I not supporting him completely in becoming a woman?

"I don't care what I wear when we're not in Key West," he'd replied, obviously annoyed by my request. "Just pick something out and throw it in the suitcase."

"Oh, come on, David; I'm not asking for much!" I was annoyed. "Don't you have any interest in what you'll wear to Christmas dinner? Could you just accommodate me a little bit?"

Our excitement about the holidays and the trip began to ebb. We'd both ended-up angry and hurt, and I'd eventually seen the deep irony in this struggle. My husband was desperate to begin living as a woman, while I was attempting to enjoy his remaining masculinity. For sixty years, his greatest desire had been to dispense with all male trappings; to don a complete feminine guise and *be* that female, evermore. Objectively, I knew what a downer this was for him; it was logical that he'd not give a damn about his male presentation.

Eventually it had occurred to me that, while most of us want to please our mates to some degree, it's an individual matter how far we will go. Perhaps there's a point at which each of us must say to the other, "I'm not willing to do that for you," as in our not-against-you-but-for-me philosophy. David had always done much to please me. But once this path to complete femininity had begun, his tolerance for being a man was running thin.

Despite this rational awareness, my emotions ruled that day, as they often did while watching my husband gradually recede. His lack of willingness to look the way I wanted him to look as a man—after years of my assistance in creating Deborah's female visage—had felt like a kick in the teeth. I'd stormed out of the bedroom in tears, fed-up with attempting to remain the supportive wife and feeling torn-apart. I wanted to promote this transition; wanted Deborah to exist at last. But I was devastated at losing my man.

My pain had multiple sources. There was my attraction to and desire for David, the man I was losing. There was also my great sadness for him, knowing the anguish he'd felt for over half a century. Plunged into grief, I'd attempted to glimpse the life we'd soon be living. It seemed that nothing would ever be the same after the transition. Certainly, the life I'd once envisioned and lived with David would be over.

What I'd felt as we packed was a wave of grief, akin to the sadness of losing my brother and sister; of ending my first marriage. I had relived the sorrow that had washed over me in the midst of my divorce, experiencing a similar heartache at losing this husband in such an odd way. I knew there would be no returning to the marriage of Leslie and David. "He" would be dead, in a way; yet, there "she" would be, still in my life. The sense of loss was familiar; but this felt like a new kind of death—a death without losing the person.

My parents had come to mind, then; their lives were so dramatically changed after Mom's polio. I thought of the depth of their love; of the deep caring and flexibility that their adjustments had required. Focusing on their strength inspired me, helping me to endure my own feelings of loss. The difference, of course, was the choice that my parents had lacked. We were actually *opting* to pursue a difficult and uncertain path, with no clear outcome. But David had been given no choice about his perplexing inner nature, and I was willing to go along with it, despite what I was giving up.

It's important to recall that I had the option of controlling the situation. For months, David had said he'd stop the transition, if only I said the word. Herein lay a paradoxical component of our relationship, that "Gift of the Magi Syndrome": He'd have been willing to forego his greatest desire, to be the husband I wanted him to be. And I, in my love and desire to support the soulful needs of my beloved, urged him on in this quest. My own heart's desire was the ultimate happiness of my mate, though I was determined this would not be to the detriment of my own long-term happiness.

I know of no more encouraging fact than the unquestionable ability of man to elevate his life by a conscious endeavor. –Henry David Thoreau

CHAPTER THIRTEEN
COMING-OUT IN THE NEW YEAR, 2011

JOURNAL ENTRY: Tomorrow is our service at church and D can hardly wait. S/he's past ready to come-out to our fellow parishioners, fed-up with living a lie in our dear little church. I think these people will love and support us, and I'm glad to demonstrate my support for my spouse. Mostly, I'm glad D will have the relief of revealing this secret to people we know so well, as he's getting somewhat desperate to proceed. This all seems surreal to me most of the time, so I'm basically ready for anything!

THE JANUARY DAY OF OUR service arrived. There'd be no turning back now. Deborah and I entered the church community hall, where a few folks had arrived early to prepare for the coffee hour which follows the service. They knew that our homily was entitled "Slaying Our Dragons" and that it would be presented by the Fabians, but we'd purposely omitted our first names from the program, as well as anything about the substance of our talk. Trickling toward us to say hello, they undoubtedly wondered why I was there without David—and who the tall, thin woman accompanying me might be.

Recognition was lacking until one woman, looking puzzled, asked Deb, "Are you David's sister?"

I knew this thrilled my spouse. It meant she was really able to pass as a woman. But as soon as Debby said, "Well, no, actually, I'm David," our friend recognized his voice and realized her error. (Speaking is frequently the give-away for Ts who pass

70

well in appearance.) In her surprise, this woman then pointed to Deborah's breasts, chuckling. "Well, those aren't real then, are they?"

Despite our shock, we told her that the breasts were, indeed, very real. David's fifteen months on female hormones and testosterone blocker had produced this desired effect. This was the kind of awkward moment that we knew would recur, so we'd been determined to develop thick skin for what was to come. We headed upstairs, to set-up for our service, leaving a wake of astonished parishioners.

The service soon began with the usual format of announcements, hymns, silent reflection, the collection. Then came our homily, with my introduction:

For those of you new to Unitarian-Universalism, this is the church where we can suggest that God just might be a she. It's okay to say that here. So, I'll quote Anne Lemott who suggests, tongue-in-cheek, "...if you want to make God laugh, tell her your plans!"

What we are presenting today was definitely not in the plans. You are undoubtedly shocked to observe that David is a transgender individual. [Turning to Deb] *This is Deborah. She will tell you how her plans have gone awry. As for me—well, my mother, my girlfriends, the "rulebook for life"—none ever mentioned the possibility of falling for a tall, beautiful man in a dress, eye shadow, and high heels. No doubt Spirit is having the laugh of a lifetime!*

Dragons and demons...we all have them, don't we? Big ones, small ones, quiet ones; tenacious, messy, loud ones. Niggling, insidious, and persistent, they drag us down [glance at Deb], *no pun intended! When we face and handle them, or accept and let go of the self-judgment and charge we attach to them, I believe that they can consistently strengthen and embolden us.*

For two of my three siblings, both of whom took their own lives, it seems that the demons won. I am convinced that a contributor to these tragedies was their inability to ask for help; to trust those around them to hold them up when they couldn't do it for themselves; to be there for them in ways that might have helped to save them. These senseless deaths have provided a

71

reference point for me. I ask myself, and I ask you, as well, "What can be so bad about <u>anyone</u> that that person is not lovable, worthy, and precious—and deserving of life?"

Deborah and I are here today to demonstrate our ability to ask this beloved community for support on our unusual path. Equally important is our hope that, by sharing ourselves with you in this way, we will have invited you to join us in sharing your vulnerable spots, so that we can support you as well.

I'm adjusting my plans regarding my marriage. True, this gender adventure of ours is a wild and challenging one, but my honey and I are convinced that it's worth the ride for both of us!

We know that many questions will remain unanswered today and we will gladly do our best to address them as we go forward, though we find that words fall short of explaining this mystery. Rainer Maria Rilke suggested—and Deborah and I are learning—"...to have patience with everything unresolved...and to try to love the questions themselves as if they were locked rooms or books written in a very foreign language," and to "...live [our] way into the answer."

Our future is uncertain, so Debby and I have, of necessity, made friends with ambiguity. We love this Joseph Campbell quote on a plaque on our bathroom wall: "We must be willing to let go of the life we have planned so as to have the life that is waiting for us."

In addition to whatever support you might offer us, we request that you be discerning in public with the information we are sharing today. Coming-out in this way obviously creates the possibility of wreaking havoc in our lives, especially with regard to David's medical practice. Today is not the launching of Deborah's new life; it is an experimental introduction to what lies ahead. Please be discreet and kind as you return to the community.

And now, I introduce to you my beloved Deborah!

[Deborah] Good Morning. When I am asked what Unitarian-Universalism is all about, I usually answer that it is not about what we believe, but about how we live. In this church we affirm:

72

Love is the Spirit of this church, and Service, its law. This is our great covenant:

To dwell together in peace, to seek the truth in love, and to help one another.

I like that. To me, the most important component of this worship community is the people here: How we treat each other, how we support each other, how we grow together. That is my spirituality—and you are the reason that I come here.

Some of you are probably thinking to yourselves, "Hmm; I can't quite put my finger on it, but the Fabians look a little different today." Obviously, one striking thing is Leslie's new haircut; but you probably notice something different about me, too. By coming here in this way today, I am being totally honest with all of you for the first time. Until recently, I've felt that I had to be less than fully open with you.

I have occasionally avoided coming to our services because it's so painful for me to be here and not be my true self. I've given a talk, similar to this one, at the U-U congregation in Littleton and, more recently, in Northborough. I've also presented several homilies in Provincetown as Deborah—that is, as my true self. It is time for me to be completely honest with those to whom I feel most connected: The congregation of UUSG.
[Unitarian Universalist Society of Gardner, Massachusetts]

Leslie, the most important person in my life, is here with me today. Whatever journey I am on, she is also on one of her own with this. I ask that you support her on her path as, I trust, you will support me.

If you are new to Unitarian-Universalism, I would like to give you a brief description of one of the foundations of our church. By tradition, we U-Us draw from many sources for our guidance and wisdom. We look to the transcending mystery which moves us to a renewal of the spirit. We are inspired by the words and deeds of prophetic women and men, challenging us to confront evil with the transforming power of love. We draw from the world's religions, which motivate us in our ethical and spiritual lives to respond to life's challenges by loving our neighbors as ourselves. And we are counseled by humanist teachings to heed the guidance of reason, as we are challenged by idolatries of the mind and spirit.

In keeping with this tradition, I would like to recall some of the great thoughts of a well-known amphibian source, Kermit the Frog. Kermit sings a song entitled "It's Not Easy Being Green." In it, he ponders the problems of being green; what it means to him and the struggles involved. He sings of his yearning to be some other, more acceptable color. Kermit eventually not only accepts himself in his greenness, he even comes to appreciate it. We find that we are compelled to feel compassion for Kermit's struggle and wish to walk (perhaps hop?) with him on his path to wholeness.

I stand here speaking to you this morning because I am transgender. Specifically, I am a male-to-female transsexual. And just as greenness is not easy for Kermit, it's not easy being transsexual.

I do not think it is possible for me to explain the phenomenon of transexuality in terms that will allow you to understand it. Just as I have no internal reference for what it means to be "normal," to be something other than this, you cannot have an internal reference for how it feels to be transsexual. I don't believe that any of us can experience the lives of others—the internal challenges, the dragons with which we each struggle. However, it is possible and, indeed, it is the foundation of what Unitarian-Universalism is for me, that we listen to each other and care about each others' lives.

My desire this morning is not to offer a textbook description of transgenderism. Rather, it is to tell you about my path and our personal story. There are many terms, definitions, and pronoun clarifications that I will be happy to discuss with you later. For now, I would like to make two important points about being transsexual: First, transexuality is not about whom I am attracted to, who I marry, or who I sleep with. It is about who I am and how I see myself in this world.

Second, I do not know what caused this. Transexuality may be due to a hormonal imbalance, a genetic abnormality, an anatomic or central nervous system disorder, a dysfunction in my family dynamics, or even some karmic challenge from lifetimes ago. I simply do not know.

However, I can tell you that there is one big thing that transsexuality is not: It is not a choice. I did not choose this, nor did the many friends I have in the Transgender Community choose it. It chose us. No one would have voluntarily chosen the pain that this has caused us. The only choice that I have now is whether to accept myself and live in happiness, or continue to live in hiding and shame.

I was about nine or ten when I first put on some of my sister's clothes. As I did so, I immediately knew two things: I knew that I liked it. I felt good and at ease in these clothes, a little happier while wearing them. Some part of me felt at home with this feeling, looking like this. I also knew, with much more clarity than with my first awareness, that this was very, very wrong. I knew that I should not be doing this and that I couldn't let anyone catch me. I thought that I could never reveal this to anyone.

For years, I occasionally found female clothes to put on. In them, I would feel good briefly; then guilt would overtake me. I was ashamed of my actions and desires, though I would not, could not, discuss it with anyone. I was absolutely certain that I was alone in this desire; that no one else could possibly understand. Certainly, no one else could ever accept.

When I was in medical school in the seventies, I sneaked into the psychiatry section of the library to look up transsexualism. I found that it was considered a serious psychiatric condition, affirming my need to keep it entirely to myself.

While I was doing my psychiatric rotation as a medical student, a transsexual patient had attempted suicide by jumping from a window. The teaching resident, with whom I was working, loudly commented that it was too bad he had not killed himself, since he was so highly disordered anyway. That seemed to be the belief of main-stream psychiatry at the time, and I continued to keep my secret tightly to myself.

Also in the seventies, I had my first encounter with someone while I was cross-dressed as a woman. It was the police officer who arrested, hand-cuffed, and took me to jail, simply because he saw me walking across the street in women's clothes. I was strip-searched in front of several laughing police officers, then put in a cell and told they'd be back to get my mug shots.

There was no running water in the cell, so I knelt in front of the toilet and washed off my makeup with the toilet water. That seemed preferable to being photographed while wearing makeup. However, no mug shots were ever taken, no charges were filed, as it had been determined that I'd actually broken no laws.

Later that night, I wrote myself a prescription for a large quantity of sleeping pills. I stared at the bottle for several nights, trying to decide when and how to take them. I think it was having a one-year-old daughter at home that enabled me to resist checking-out.

Two or three days later, a psychiatrist I decided to see was the next person to know of my secret. He advised me that, anytime I felt like cross-dressing, I should mentally put myself back in the jail cell. I was to relive the experience of being strip-searched; reenact the process of kneeling in front of the toilet bowl, to wash off the makeup. I took this advice, keeping the dragon partially at bay for a decade or so, as I held that image and consumed copious amounts of alcohol.

Next to be told was my now-ex-wife. She immediately labeled me "disgusting." In the past, I've been angry with her for this, but I've since realized that I did not disagree with her then; she simply confirmed what I already believed about myself. I thought that I suffered from the serious psychiatric condition about which I'd read, and shame prohibited my talking to anyone. I felt completely alone.

These days, I recommend the book She's not There: A Life in Two Genders, *by Jennifer Finney Boylan, to anyone willing to try to understand transgenderism. Ms. Boylan is a professor of English at Colby College in Maine and, like me, she is a male-to-female transsexual. As Jennifer transitioned and came out to the Colby faculty, she wrote them a letter in which she said:*

> *I have had this condition for my entire life, since before kindergarten, since before language. It is certainly a condition that I*

have had during all the years you have known me, and which has caused me an almost inexpressible degree of private grief.

The same is true for me; and, while the phrase "inexpressible degree of private grief" may seem melodramatic, I can assure you that it is not. It merely scratches the surface of my inner life.

Being transgender, for me, has been about depression. The term "yearning" comes to mind, as I think of my desire to be female. For my entire conscious life, not a day has gone by that I have not thought, at some point, that I would rather be a woman than a man. Seeing a mother holding a child, or two women in conversation, a mannequin wearing an outfit I like, or simply watching Leslie re-apply lipstick at the end of a meal—these and thousands of other common and unavoidable events have caused a longing deep inside of me. It's as if a drain plug in the pit of my stomach has been pulled, and any happiness that I may have been feeling suddenly runs out.

I have lived my life trying to resist this urge, angrily throwing away clothes many times, as if they were the enemy. I have often wondered what other men feel and I've tried to act as they do, but it feels unnatural to me. I have attempted to be open with others about myself, yet the deepest yearning inside of me has, until recent years, been unspeakable.

In the summer of 1986, I finally found and began therapy with a woman who specializes in transgenderism. Niela Miller was the first person in my life who could be told my inner feelings—and she did not find me disgusting. She actually showed me that I wasn't alone.

That October, Niela urged me to go to Provincetown, Massachusetts, for a week-long event: Fantasia Fair. At this annual gathering, there were at least 150 transgender people, some accompanied by partners and spouses. This was the first time I'd allowed myself to be cross-dressed in the presence of others, except for the ill-fated excursion that had ended in my arrest. I was petrified, paranoid, and afraid of my own shadow.

One evening at the Fair, I dressed for an event, convinced that I looked something like the Incredible Hulk in drag! I walked downstairs in my bed and breakfast, passing through the living room. There, on the couch, with their arms around each other, was the gay couple who managed the inn. I was shocked. I had never knowingly talked to a gay couple before, and I'd certainly never witnessed affection like this between two men. I became extremely uncomfortable, recalling homophobic slurs my father had used in my childhood.

I left the house and walked toward my event, gradually becoming aware of the irony of that encounter. Here I was, in my most vulnerable state: Dressed as a woman, afraid of the world, struggling even to accept myself. I suddenly realized that I was asking them to accept me for who I was, though I'd not done the same for them.

I turned around, returned to that living room, and the three of us talked about my experience for over an hour. Although I'm no longer in touch with those men, the memory of our encounter has been instrumental in my life. I'd learned that accepting myself necessarily means finding a way to accept others.

I met Leslie at a workshop at my therapist's house in 1987, and I was cross-dressed at the time. This spring, we will celebrate our twentieth wedding anniversary and, although our path together has never been without bumps, I've discovered something akin to unconditional love. Leslie wants me to be happy; wants me to be true to myself. She loves me as I am, and I hope that she receives something like this from me.

Now, if this were a fairy tale, it would go something like this: I was cured of my unnatural urges and Leslie and I have lived happily ever after. That is not the case, however. Leslie and I are doing wonderfully, but I have not been cured.

For most of my life, I thought that if only I could cross-dress occasionally, I would be perfectly happy. In my twenty years with Leslie, I've been able to do that. Yet, depression has continued to come and go. About a year-and-a-half ago, it became apparent that therapy sessions and antidepressants were providing only partial, temporary relief, at best. Leslie was clearly getting tired of dealing with me. She alternated between anger and sadness for me, as she witnessed my elation during a week at Fantasia Fair or an evening at dinner as Deborah. Then she'd watch me fall back into a state of depression as we returned home to the other life.

I, too, became tired of me. At the suggestion of a life coach, Janet Parker, I began a series of workshops in creativity and improvisational acting, led by a wonderful therapist-coach-actor, Daena Giardella. Dressed as Deborah, I attended these classes weekly and had my first experience of an on-going social life as a woman. The classes were intended for creativity and theatrical training; for me, they were truly therapeutic and transformational.

In one class, as I re-created the scene of my 1976 arrest, I had a stroke of awareness. I realized that the painful episodes in my life, the events that caused me to be disgusted with myself, had occurred decades before. In recent years, as I've explored my transgenderism, I've actually received only acceptance, support, and caring.

I also noticed that the best part of each week was as I dressed, prepared for, drove to, then attended my class. This was the time I could spend as the person I really am. The worst time in my week was at the end of each evening, as I undressed. I'd regularly dip into significant depression, knowing that it would be another week before the real me could reemerge. I eventually realized that I could not go through the rest of my life without having what I have most wanted. I needed to be myself—to become Deborah.

Just over a year ago, with Leslie's strong support, I decided that I needed to start taking female hormones. This was not an easy decision. I could think of a thousand reasons why I shouldn't do this and only one reason why I should: Because it felt right.

I began estrogen therapy in the fall of 2009. This was a major commitment to my future, though I was not at all sure I would continue it. As I swallowed the first pill, however—before the first Premarin molecule hit my blood stream—I felt my sadness begin to lift. Now, each day as I take the medication, I pause to ask myself if this is what I want to do. The answer has never been anything less than a resounding "Yes!"

I am delighted by the physical and emotional changes that are occurring. Amazingly, I feel happy now for longer than ever before. In fact, I'm happier than I have ever been. This is the right decision for me. As I told Leslie recently, "I like feeling happy."

Today I am able to say to you and, perhaps more importantly, I'm able to say to myself:

My spiritual self is female; my sense of self in community is that of female. I am most happy and most at ease when I allow myself to present as female. Now I wish to bring my outer self into harmony with my inner spirit.

I'm sure there will be challenges and obstacles to overcome, but the pain that this transition may cause will be far less than what I'd experience if I didn't take this path. And Leslie is with me for the journey.

Jennifer Finney Boylan says in She's Not There:

> *...we all have dragons to slay in life. This one is mine. I hope that doing so will provide a model to others on how to find the bravery to be true to oneself, even if it means doing something that seems impossible.*

I do not pretend to be a model of bravery for anyone. I have stumbled my way to this point in my life. But perhaps this church community can be a model to the world: Of acceptance, tolerance, support, and healing, for anyone attempting to slay her own dragon. This is my dragon, the part of me that most needs the healing of this place.

—Namaste and Blessed Be —

There was an immediate standing ovation. This had occurred each time Deborah had given this talk—and here was *our* congregation, on their feet! We knew that most folks had been stunned, first by David's presence in so changed a form; then by the moving story of his transgender life. Yet, it already seemed clear that they were ready to lend their support.

We completed the service with readings and a hymn and were then embraced by these compassionate people. There were hugs and congratulations, expressions of concern. They asked how I was doing; they asked what they could do to help us. With tears in many eyes, they told us how moved they were, and they wondered how David had lived for so long with this enormous burden. We were encircled by loving kindness that persisted through our coffee hour, as we continued to explain this journey on which we'd embarked.

Soon, word was out about the transition among the Unitarian-Universalists in our area. David's willingness to dress as Deborah and speak to these Massachusetts congregations had led to multiple Sunday morning engagements. They were well received by congregants and much enjoyed by my spouse.

In the spring, a U-U minister in a neighboring town had requested something different. She wanted both of us to present for a service called "Standing on the Side of Love." I'd participated in church services with Deb (and David) several times before, but this would be the first in which we would share the homily.

It was exciting to prepare; to dissect our relationship and examine how we were maintaining it, in spite of our unusual circumstances. Several days before the service, we'd met with the minister for some coaching. She'd asked us something quite simple, yet profound: "What do you love about each other?"

This was a slight variation on what I first posit with couples who see me for couple's counseling, though it's not something David and I had asked ourselves for some time. It was a great way to get us focused on why we're together and what we wanted to say in the service. The morning after our meeting, I'd awakened thinking about our presentation and what I wanted to say, and suddenly found myself in tears of wonder and gratitude. Still groggy, lying in bed, I had realized that there are innumerable things that I love about my mate. As I considered the minister's question, I'd thought: What's *not* to love?

For this service, we spoke alternately, presenting facets of our lives and relationship. Deborah contributed her typical story, always so moving; I added components of our lives not yet revealed in a church. Parts of our service bear repeating, though much of what we said had been told before. I began:

We've been invited to talk to you today as a couple who are Standing on the Side of Love, despite rather extraordinary circumstances. Presumably, we have something unique in this marriage of ours, something useful or inspiring that we might impart to you. There is no question that there is a uniqueness to at least one of us. That's my husband, David, over there! [Gesturing to Deborah, on the opposite side] *I guess I'm somewhat unusual, too. I am someone committed to being true to myself, and I've always encouraged my beloved to do this, as well. Now I'm supporting him in becoming who he has longed to be for most of his life. I'm also reasonably certain that we will remain married, despite this major transition.*

There are many women who are aware that they are married to cross-dressers. Yet, even those who willingly accept this uncommon proclivity often live in fear that their husbands may someday want to become women. Though I never believed this would come to pass for my spouse, I also never feared it. Truth be told, I'd prefer to be married to David: A man who occasionally likes dressing as a woman. But we've concluded that this is not to be. After heading in this direction for about a year-and-a-half, my spouse is vividly aware that there's no turning back now. And I know, in my soul, that it's not for me to deny this change. I'm every bit as aware as Deborah that this transition must proceed.

David and I were married in 1991, beginning an odyssey that seems to encompass dramatic change, frequent challenge, and rich opportunities for discovery and growth. We intentionally practice acceptance, self-awareness, respect, forgiveness, and active loving in our relationship. We believe that we've created what Dr. Harville Hendrix calls a "conscious marriage." We are continuing to grow in our loving and devotion to one another, even as David morphs into Deborah.

Near the end of our homily, Deb gave voice to her gratitude for my loving support, honoring me and our relationship before this new congregation, saying:

Our talk this morning is about love, something I've needed to learn how to give and, equally important, to receive. Despite my deep love for Leslie and hers for me, my self-loathing sometimes stood in the way of reaching-out to her in the ways that I wanted; to express to her what I felt deep inside. Now that I'm free to be who I truly am, I am able to love her with greater honesty and openness than ever before.

[Turning to me] Leslie, you, quite literally, saved my life. You saw, in me, a depth I hadn't glimpsed in myself, and you've helped me to blossom and grow. People often toss-out the term "unconditional love." As the U-U minister who married us said in our ceremony, "I've never met anyone who loves unconditionally. However, you two come very close."

I wish for you, my love, to have the very best in our relationship. I've learned that, in order to be most present and available to you and to our marriage, I must be whole. During the years that I've struggled for wholeness, I've also endeavored to accept you, fully, for all that you are. I've learned that the little things that have sometimes annoyed me are, in fact, just that: Little things.

In her book, She's Not There, *Jennifer Finney Boylan talks about her battle with the dragon of transsexualism. She had hoped, as I have, that this constant desire to be female would go away; that this overwhelming need would disappear, leaving her in peace. Like me, she found that there was nothing she could do to make it disappear. One day, she'd had a vision, imagining that, in her words, "...love will cure me."*

Well, I think that love <u>has</u> cured me, but not in the way I'd expected. It didn't rid me of this need; it cured me in a much deeper way. Love has allowed me to be my whole self, to express my deepest needs, and to become who I have always felt myself to be. Love and Leslie walk the path toward wholeness with me.

I wrapped-up our presentation, telling these folks that the process of preparing to appear before them had provided me with additional encouragement to continue this journey with Deborah:

Well, I'm now writing a book about our story and find that this creative process is immensely powerful in helping me to accept the impending change. I also found new confirmation for handling the transition when I woke up the other morning, thinking of what I wanted to say today. I focused on your minister's question to us: "What do you two love about each other?" I realized I can't even begin to list the things that I love about this person and our marriage. They are countless!

I adore my spouse and the beautiful, precious, vulnerable soul that had shown-through that first evening in 1987. I cannot imagine attempting to squelch her movement toward fulfillment and joy, and I can hardly entertain the possibility of leaving so rich and gratifying a bond as ours. Every day, we see how this journey strengthens us, individually and as a couple. We acknowledge the difficulties, the plethora of unknowns, and, especially, the amazing joy of Standing on the Side of Love.

— Namaste and Blessed Be —

Never take counsel of your fears. –Andrew Jackson

∾

CHAPTER FOURTEEN
OUR FEARS ARISE—WHAT NEXT?

JOURNAL ENTRY: God, how much easier this transition would be if there wasn't a society out there that frowns on this. It's still difficult for gays, lesbians, and bisexual folks, and we're dealing with the "T" [of "GLBT"]. Not just the "simple form," either—cross-dressing, in private or otherwise—but a man becoming a woman. D is a beautiful, tender, caring, brilliant man, choosing to honor <u>her</u> soul and change genders. Why does it have to be so difficult? What difference can it make in anyone else's life?

∾

One profound result of our Gardner service was that it had led to the complete reversal of thinking on the part of David's primary care physician [PCP], Dr. John Harrington. While supporting the transition before he'd heard Deborah speak, he had thought it doubtful that Deborah would be able to continue practicing orthopedics in Gardner.

Until the fall of 2009, John had known nothing of David's transgenderism. We'd informed him together early-on, since he'd be receiving medical records from the Boston endocrinologist. Trepidation over revealing the situation was magnified by the fact that the two men were colleagues, and John would be the first of his fellow docs to be informed of David's plan. It had felt like a huge risk to expose this secret. Nevertheless, he was a trusted professional and had to be told.

John's response to our story exemplified why he is so beloved a member of the community; why David had chosen him as his PCP. He listened with patience and compassion, then gave each of us a bear hug, telling David, "You know, you're not just my patient; you're my colleague and friend. This doesn't change anything for me. I'm honored to help you with your transition."

We were elated. Another hurdle had been cleared as the gradual revelation of the transition began. However, John had soon erected another roadblock, despite his compassionate caring. Shortly after we'd told him the plan, David explored John's thinking on whether Deborah might maintain a successful orthopedic practice in Gardner. Our concerns centered mostly on our impressions of the area and its demographics.

Gardner is a small manufacturing city of approximately 21,000 in north central Massachusetts. It's about sixty miles from Boston and thirty miles from Worcester, the Commonwealth's second largest city. We were doubtful that Gardner was large or urbane enough to accept one of its male surgeons becoming a woman.

Since Dr. Harrington knew the people and conditions here—he'd practiced in the area for nearly thirty years—there was good reason to trust his assessment. He clearly held the utmost respect for David's work as a surgeon and reiterated his steadfast support for the transition; but he affirmed our belief that Gardner was not the environment in which a transsexual might make such a change and continue to practice medicine with success. Accepting John's opinion, David resumed looking at jobs elsewhere, a process he'd actually initiated several months earlier.

When he'd begun the female hormones, we feared that the transition would necessitate finding a new location in which to practice. We assumed that Deborah would be more readily accepted in or near a larger city, where this sort of thing might be less extraordinary. By the fall of 2010, David had been in touch with a number of medical recruiters, including two who'd advertised jobs in Key West and Hawaii—enticing possibilities. He'd been forthright in telling each recruiter about his transsexualism and the plan to transition before joining a new practice.

During our Christmas holiday in Key West, he'd attempted to contact the CEO at the Florida hospital, hoping to tour the facility and meet some of the personnel; but the communication had been strictly one-way. Despite several calls, the CEO did not call back or even have her assistant contact us. We'd thought this disrespectful and rude, and it exacerbated our concerns about the impact of the transition on our livelihood.

We heard nothing more about the Key West job, nor did the recruiter for the Hawaii job follow-up. By the beginning of 2011, it was clear that these recruiters, as well as several others David had contacted, had lost interest in assisting the transitioning transsexual. Clearly, this monumental change would have an impact on every facet of our lives.

∞

Whether confidentiality had been broken at the Gardner hospital, we'll never know; but word had been leaking-out that something strange was happening with Dr. Fabian. He'd been revealing his transition plans, in confidence, to a growing number of people there, mentioning that we'd probably be moving away. Surprisingly, despite John Harrington's doubts, everyone else at the hospital who was told was encouraging him to stay. It was evident that he was loved, respected, and admired as a human being and a surgeon: Easy to work with, skilled, and funny. I knew that he was also well-liked and appreciated by many patients; I'd been hearing this the entire time we'd been together.

In particular, one anesthesiologist and several operating room nurses were practically begging him to stay. They'd repeatedly told him, "We know you here and we love you. We don't want to lose you. Why would you want to go somewhere else and start all over again? We'll support you through this. Please don't leave!"

This was heart-warming and encouraging (though, of course, the ones with whom David had shared the secret were those he'd assumed would be supportive). There were many others who might not be so receptive to this transformation; some might reject it outright, as the recruiters had. Furthermore, there was a huge difference between being supportive of the transition, as John Harrington had been, and accepting Deborah professionally.

We were inclined to rely on Dr. Harrington's counsel and continue looking elsewhere, though jobs were not manifesting. If we stayed in Gardner and the orthopedic practice shrank, we'd be moving on—but to where? To what? There was no way to predict either the outcome of remaining here or just who might decide to take-on the transsexual surgeon.

∞

On the day of our U-U service, John had been there for the homily but had needed to leave before we finished. We'd had no idea how the service had affected him until he called later that day, and his response was remarkable. John told David how moved he had been, witnessing Deborah in person and hearing the poignant story. He had reached a different conclusion about the viability of our remaining in the area and, in addition to his professional support as David's physician, he vowed to go to bat with the medical community. John was prepared to convince them of the wisdom of supporting their transitioned colleague in remaining among them. Amazingly, he was now determined to ensure that the hospital would not lose this outstanding orthopedic surgeon.

We were completely awed by John's change of perspective, his change of heart. Something about what had been said, perhaps the way in which we'd presented it, had convinced him that this odd and mysterious transition might actually work in our small Massachusetts community. He'd also seen David—as Deborah—for the first time that day. I believe this is a key to many people's acceptance. Before seeing her, they might conjure outrageous images of my masculine husband as a female. But the fact is, Deborah looked good!

*Excellence is the Result of Caring more than
others think is Wise, Risking more than others think is Safe,
Dreaming more than others think is Practical,
and Expecting more than others think is Possible.* –Ronnie Oldham

∞

CHAPTER FIFTEEN
IT'S TIME TO DO THIS ALL THE WAY

JOURNAL ENTRY: OMG! We have so much going-on right now! Fortunately, we're feeling really close and are excited about all the change that's happening. This afternoon we head to Connecticut so David can meet the docs at the hospital, to tell them about the transition. The job is secured and he's not required to meet with them, but he wants to inform them beforehand that he will be "somewhat changed" when starting work there in the fall. He's been rehearsing possible scenarios, has read *Getting to Yes*, and we've imagined every outcome that we can. He's ready!

We've decided to put the house on the market. In fact, our realtor insisted. It's hardly ready for showing, but we're leaving for Ireland and the UK in two days, and summer is the season for selling houses. Somehow we also need to find time to pack for our twelve days away.

∞

ONCE WE HAD JOHN HARRINGTON'S commitment to assist with Deborah's remaining in Gardner, we were optimistic about this possibility. Still, David continued to look at other jobs. He'd been practicing orthopedics for nearly thirty years and had a strong desire to cut back on his hours and the need to be on-call so frequently. Retirement was out of the question; we still had some large financial commitments. Besides, he loved the work.

One of the challenges in the job search, now that there'd been multiple rejections, was deciding who needed to be informed of the impending gender change and when to tell them. Since it hadn't worked to be up-front with recruiters (they'd disappear after being told the transition plans; or they'd say that the position had been filled or withdrawn), David was creating job search methods as he went along. It was tricky to determine how to proceed.

By spring of 2011, it seemed that the best bet for being hired might be to skip telling the transition news to recruiters, waiting to speak directly with the physicians and hospital personnel at the job site. There was no question that Dr. Fabian—David *or* Deborah—would be an asset to any orthopedic position. His training, credentials, and experience, including a stint as Chief of Surgery in Framingham, Massachusetts, were impeccable. None of that would alter in any way because of the transition.

An amazing opportunity materialized: A job in a Connecticut hospital that seemed ideal for the years leading up to our retirement. The position was as an orthopedic hospitalist, on-call for emergencies for ten straight, twenty-four hour days each month. Then, the rest of each month we'd be free! This demanding schedule is doable, with physicians' assistants at the hospital handling late-night emergencies. Naturally, we were enthralled at this prospect.

The hiring process went beautifully, with David being chosen by the North Carolina recruiting company for one of three positions to be filled. By late spring, he'd flown south and signed a contract with this company, which acted as an agent for the hospital. All that remained was to meet the Connecticut hospital physicians—a mere technicality, really; the job was already his.

Of course, at this meeting, he'd explain that there would be a considerable variation in his appearance and a name change, too. We were hopeful; things seemed to be going well. Practically giddy with the anticipated freedom that the new job promised, we looked forward to the entirety of our next great adventure.

Then, between the contract-signing in North Carolina and the up-coming Connecticut interview, I became terrified for our future security. I'd visited long-time friends, sans David, and excitedly told them our plans. They'd raised the proverbial red flag: "What if the hospital doesn't buy it? Suppose they balk and find a way to cancel the contract. How will you two maintain the lifestyle you enjoy if there's no job?"

As they'd pointed-out, not only did we have a lifestyle we wanted to preserve, we had the legal obligation of alimony and the balance of a mortgage on a home we'd built in Nebraska. What if we proceeded as planned and closed the Gardner practice, lost the CT job, and found that Deborah was unable to generate an income? This would be disastrous.

These were not negative folks who'd simply wanted to rain on our parade; they were caring friends, concerned about us. I told them of our apprehension about staying in Gardner, should the Connecticut job fall through, and they'd asked whether we had a plan for back-up, in case neither situation worked out. This suddenly felt like a much-needed reality check; a real dope slap to a couple of dopes.

We'd neglected to contemplate a need for anything beyond our two plans; had not considered that a time might come when we'd need a whole list of plans. My natural optimism and that old deceiver, denial, had pacified us into ignoring realistic concerns that we should be considering. I'd been colluding in this recklessness with David, who was so joyful at finally transitioning.

I guess Dr. Harrington's encouragement, and the small group at the hospital, who'd been attempting to persuade David to remain in Gardner, had soothed us into believing that we could definitely stay there, if need-be. There was a glitch to this, however: David was not a hospital employee; he had a private practice with hospital privileges, but no guaranteed salary. If patients were too uncomfortable after David transitioned to Deborah, they'd stop coming-in and our income would vanish.

With my friends playing devil's advocates, we'd done some brain-storming and a logical plan emerged. Agreeing that the hospitalist position was a dream job, not to be jeopardized, we wondered whether David might remain his male-self during the ten days per month in Connecticut, then live as Deborah for the rest of each month. Wouldn't this ensure that the Connecticut job remained intact?

I'd returned home from my visit, prepared to confront David with my newly-formed fears and a reasonable argument. I was pretty sure he'd resist the plan, formulated without his input, but I had to let him know how scared I'd become. What ensued was a very unpleasant exchange.

I began my bargaining efforts by relating the concerns that our friends had raised and asking my husband, "Couldn't you do a gradual transition over these next few years before you retire? You've been David for over sixty years; you know how to do that. Rather than risk losing this job, can't you just do it as you are? Then we can go anywhere and live however we want for the rest of the month. It makes perfect sense!"

David was really aggravated to hear that we'd been discussing him and our plans without his participation. "Don't they know I've considered all that?" he'd angrily asked. "What do people think I've been losing sleep over and worrying about for most of my life?"

"But this is scaring me, David! I just don't think we should take the chance," I'd argued. "You know they can find a way to oust you once you tell them about the transition. What happens if your income stops? You know I can't support our lifestyle!"

I'd told him how frightened I was, imagining him (her) with no job at all, and he had theorized, "If living as Deborah doesn't work, I'll go back to being David again."

"I don't believe you for a minute! If you start living as Deborah, you'll never be able to go back. I know you too well. That's not going to happen!"

He'd been adamant then, telling me, "Forget it! It's time to do this all the way and I'm not waiting any longer. I won't even consider it."

I vividly recall what transpired next: A wave of near-hysteria on my part, for starters. In pain, fear, and utter frustration, I'd charged out of the house and dropped down on our front stoop, bursting into tears. My mind was racing as I wept, reviewing my life, so full of unexpected challenges that I'd had to overcome. Then I'd begun to laugh at these circumstances, thinking: *How can all of this happen in one little lifetime? What next, God? What else am I in for?* (As if I'd get some clue as to what was to come!)

I don't recall ever having cried and laughed simultaneously as I did then. But, fortunately, the rational, observing part of me gradually reengaged. I recognized that the fuel for this outburst was my feeling that *everything* was out-of-my-hands. Nothing seemed in my control at that moment; perhaps nothing was.

I calmed down and saw what I needed to do: Determine when I'm being inappropriately controlling; figure out how to correct myself when I'm trying too hard to direct things; know when I'm being sensible and wise, not just controlling; then present my viewpoint without attacking or belittling my mate. I also needed to maintain my gentleness with *myself*; this uncharted escapade of ours had no precedent and would continue to be crazy-making.

Ultimately, I'd conceded to David and his forceful declarations, despite my fear and misgivings. He had reached the limits of self-denial; he'd no longer put the transition on-hold. After decades of denying what he most truly wanted, my mate was taking a firm stand, committed and immovable. I managed to bury my concerns and continue to admire his boldness and conviction, the steadfastness of his life-long dream. I opted to accept what he'd declared, "Trust me; I know I can make this happen."

With the contract signed for the Connecticut job, we decided to put our house on the market that June, assuming we'd soon have the luxury of traveling at-will or settling anywhere we desired. If we were some distance from Connecticut, Deborah would simply fly there for those ten working days each month. The house wasn't ready for showing, but our realtor pushed us to market it, to take advantage of the best selling season.

After the multiple recruiters and possible jobs had disappeared, David had wisely engaged a Connecticut lawyer to guide him through the hiring process. This man had proposed that David *not* inform the CT hospital staff, but simply show-up for work as Deborah. He'd said there was no legal reason to reveal the future identity, and Deb would (obviously) arrive with the identical background. This did not sit well with my husband, however; revelation felt essential to being aligned with his integrity.

We'd signed a contract with our realtor, and David was scheduled to meet with the folks at the hospital in just three days. Two days later, we were departing for a twentieth anniversary trip to Ireland, Scotland, and England. There were four impressive letters of recommendation to present in Connecticut, two from long-time Gardner physicians, two more from operating room nurses. They'd all "met" Deborah and recommended her with a single reservation: They'd be losing one of their favorite surgeons.

We had just five days to prepare our house for showing before we'd leave the country, and the need to pack for a twelve-day trip; but I'd still felt compelled to accompany David to Connecticut. I wanted to be there to support him, in case the meeting did not go well. He was nervous, but prepared, having practiced for every conceivable reaction.

The weekend before, I had read aloud from *Getting to Yes,* by Roger Fisher, William Ury, and Bruce Patton. These authors provide techniques for creating win-win solutions, and David wanted to utilize every possible method for this sort of outcome. We knew the Connecticut folks were pleased with his credentials, expertise, and experience; there was simply the need to tell them of the up-coming transition, affirming that Deborah would be just as desirable as David.

Meeting consecutively with two groups of three physicians, David had twice needed to make the difficult announcement about his impending change. Both times it was met by a brief stunned silence, then by what appeared to be complete acceptance and encouragement. I had thought it crucial to show them a photo of Deborah, as everyone's imagination would certainly conjure an unflattering image of David in drag. But when he'd offered it, no one expressed a desire to see the photo, nor did they care to read the letters of recommendation. It had simply seemed not to be an issue. After our weeks of careful preparation, practice, and an apparent overabundance of apprehension, this Connecticut hospital seemed prepared to have a transsexual surgeon on-board.

We were ecstatic on our two-hour drive back home, stopping for a celebratory dinner and toasting our success. Within a day, David was contacted by the lone African-American surgeon at the meetings to congratulate him and welcome him on-board. He'd told David how impressed he was by his courage, adding that he'd also called the recruiter to convey his pleasure with their choice. Two days later, still euphoric, we'd left for our twelve days of play in Ireland and the UK.

Our happy future seemed assured, but as we'd traveled abroad and celebrated our twenty-year marriage and David's new position, the forces of fear and discrimination had been churning back in the States. We could only guess, later, whether the turmoil was at the hospital in New England, the North Carolina search firm, or some combination of fearful individuals from north and south.

Back home in July 2011, we needed specifics about the Connecticut job, as we knew only that it would begin in the fall. Before we'd be ready to leave Gardner, there was office staff to inform, patients to be notified, a medical practice to be closed, and a hospital that would need to replace Dr. Fabian. Yet, despite multiple calls to each, neither the Connecticut hospital nor the recruiters were getting back to David. In spite of the signed contract and the positive responses, it began to feel much like the previous instances of disregard by recruiters.

Amazingly, upon returning from our trip, we'd been met with a reasonable offer to buy our house. In just two weeks, a young couple had found their dream house and wanted to buy our lovely antique. Everything was going so well; why weren't we hearing about the job?

Finally, ten days after our return, word came from the recruiting company that the hospital was rescinding the job offer. Despite the signed contract and former good tidings all-around, they'd trumped up two absurd reasons for dumping Deb.

First, probably due to an impulsive, humorous comment he'd made, disdaining late-night trips to the emergency room, they'd decided that Dr. Fabian would be unable to handle the pressure of late-night emergencies. They thought he'd be disagreeable with their patients. This, after thirty years of practice, with nary a complaint regarding his handling of the obligation. Their reasoning was anything but reasonable.

The other bogus issue was probably based on David's telling them that, while I owned a laptop computer, he didn't have one of his own. He'd need to buy one for himself; then he'd have access to x-rays in a hotel room, without needing to go into the hospital. Incredibly, they'd concluded this meant that he was unable to *use* a computer, though we'd had a desktop at home for years and there were multiple electronic devices in his office. They'd determined, laughably, that this accomplished surgeon would be unable to master their new electronic record-keeping system, though it was not even installed at the hospital at the time of the interview. No one there was familiar with it before its installation. Once it was set up, the staff would all be trained to use the system.

When told of these phony allegations, David knew immediately what was occurring. Once again, it had been decided that a male-to-female orthopedic surgeon, one of impeccable reputation and skill, was simply too bizarre for their taste. Here was blatant discrimination, so thinly veiled as to be completely ludicrous.

David learned that the job had evaporated when he was at home, alone, in Massachusetts. I was at the cabin, in New Hampshire, when he called with the news: "The Goddamned recruiter finally returned my call. I can't believe it! The hospital decided they don't want me after all. And they had the recruiter call me to do their dirty work!"

"Oh, my God, Honey! What'd he say? How can they do this?" I was as shocked as he.

"You won't believe what they came up with! They're trying to base it on things I told them in the interview. It's ridiculous! Things like how I'll handle being on-call in the middle of the night. I've never had a complaint in my entire career! And, would you believe, they think I can't handle their friggin' electronic record-keeping system? I guess it's because I told them I've been avoiding it in Gardner. But we were all joking and laughing about this stuff! They knew I was kidding. Nobody took it seriously!"

We had quickly agreed that we'd not let the hospital—or the recruiters, who'd colluded in the hospital's falsities, claiming that David had not actually been one of their first choices!—get away with this appalling behavior without consequences. We knew there were grounds for a lawsuit, charging discrimination against my spouse.

At this point in our conversation, David was on the verge of exploding or falling apart, maybe both. He was too devastated to continue talking and needed to end the call. I knew he was in a state of shock and despair. Sympathizing as best I could, I'd assured him of my support for moving-on to whatever came next, reiterating my love and commitment to the transition plans, regardless.

I'd been ineffective in comforting David; the news was too fresh, too raw. I hung up and began digesting the information, contemplating the significance of this latest turn of events. Soon, I was outraged at the cowardice of these people. I fumed at the stupidity of what they'd done. Not only had they lost the opportunity to have an exceptionally dedicated, skilled, and integral surgeon on their staff, they'd eschewed the chance to employ some progressive thinking and demonstrate their commitment to what they claimed on their website: ...*we recognize the value of workforce diversity and the opportunities it can bring. ...We're proud to have created an environment that draws upon the varied backgrounds of individuals from all walks of life. ...We are an equal opportunity/affirmative action employer.* Apparently, they would decide what *type* of diversity would be welcomed on their hospital staff.

I recalled how I'd begged David, a couple months earlier, to handle the situation differently; of his telling me to trust him, that he'd make it work. I'd yielded to his assurances, hoping for the best, choosing to accept our fate. Well, here was fate: He hadn't made it work and he'd lost the chance.

I was pissed and bitter! Angry at myself, I'd thought: *What the hell made you think that David could make it work, Leslie? It wasn't really up to him; it was entirely in the hands of those idiots at the hospital!*

Then I was enraged that he'd actually believed he was in charge of the outcome; that he'd absurdly imagined he could make it happen. Again, I berated myself: "How could you have been so passive, Leslie? You just went right along with his ridiculous belief!"

Finally, my anger and disappointment began to fall squarely on the individuals who were altering our lives in this outrageous way. "How could they do this? How can they treat David this way? What about our lives, our livelihood? They're not going to get away with this!"

I'd spent the rest of that evening alternately weeping and raging, while trying to figure it all out. I was glad for my own space to behave like a raving lunatic, while David struggled with his misery back at home. We were both so distressed; I doubt either of us was sane enough to be of much help to the other.

The next day, after a fitful, mostly sleepless night, David contacted the Connecticut lawyer. It was time to ramp-up his legal function, to explore how best to deal with this inexcusable retraction. Our lawyer advised that the first step would be filing a complaint with the Connecticut Commission on Human Rights and agreed to start the proceedings.

When David and I talked that evening, we tried to recall whether we'd ever experienced anything like this before. We realized we'd reached our sixties without encountering flagrant discrimination such as this. Our empathy swelled for those who live with bigotry—not just once, but all their lives. Now we were dealing with a massive dose of it ourselves.

We began preparing to fight a legal battle, to dash this injustice and make a statement that would be heard far and wide, hoping to help others, as well as ourselves. There'd been far too much discrimination against transgendered people, many who lacked the means to pursue it legally. We knew we could afford to do something about it, and decided we couldn't afford not to.

Of course, we now needed to decide whether to revert to Plan B—attempting to stay in Gardner—or quickly devise the Plan C we'd neglected to create. Our lives were growing ever more convoluted and complex.

Challenges make you discover things about yourself that you never really knew. They're what make the instrument stretch— what make you go beyond the norm. –Cicely Tyson

∞

CHAPTER SIXTEEN
WHAT'S IN THIS FOR ME?

JOURNAL ENTRY: I'll be sixty in a month and I'm astonished at how fine this feels! I'm comfortable with middle-age and this comfort feels almost like an accomplishment. I think I finally believe—truly, deeply, in my soul—that I am loved; that I am, indeed, a perfect creation of God, even with all my flaws. Sometimes I forget this. But when I remember, I know that I am enlightened and truly free.

∞

THE DIFFICULTY THAT HAD ARISEN during our packing for Key West had exemplified a frequent struggle for me. During the two transition years, fall of 2009 to fall of 2011, I'd realized I was dealing with the predictable stages of grief and loss put forth by Dr. Elisabeth Kubler-Ross, in 1969. These five stages— Denial/Isolation, Anger, Bargaining, Depression, and Acceptance—are seen in dying individuals, as well as those who survive them. The theory also extends to include those who undergo life-threatening or life-altering events. This transition was clearly of the life-altering kind.

I reviewed what I'd learned about grief and loss, finding it helpful to identify what stage was occurring with me. The recognition helped me to accept whatever I was experiencing. There was the typical over-lapping of stages and erratic nature of the process, with no one stage remaining in place for long and recurrences of stages I'd already felt. I'd already had multiple variations of this grief process, first with my brother's death; with my dissolving marriage; then my sister's suicide; and, finally, my parents' deaths. I was no stranger to losing something precious.

I had little concern for the depression stage, though I certainly knew to watch for it. I'd endured three clinical depressions, between 1972 and 1993, each (blessedly) shorter and less profound than the last. Through those years, I had learned a great deal about caring for myself in ways that have prevented my sinking to that depth of despair again. And, as a clinician who'd suffered depression herself, I had altered my viewpoint regarding the condition. I'd begun to see it as a necessary process, for some of us, in the evolution of the soul, the higher self. This allowed me to accept my emotions and love myself through them, rather than lengthening my difficulties by chastising myself and hating the feelings.

My grief in the transition years was accompanied, paradoxically, by celebrating with David as he became the woman he'd always wanted to be. There was no question that I was losing my husband. Yet, there'd be no physical death to endure, and I'd never seen him so happy for so long. Therein lay my greatest struggle: Supporting something that was desirable to me, only in that it meant fulfillment and happiness for my mate.

I seemed to skip stage one of the grief process, that of Denial and Isolation. I think that denial had actually taken place throughout most of our years together, as I'd so often witnessed David's longing to sustain the feminine role and his extreme grief at returning to masculinity. Had we both been denying all the signals that a change was needed? If denial was present during the two transition years, it was likely in those moments when I thought this might be just a dream from which I'd eventually awaken.

I certainly did not feel isolated from David. His support and love for me as he transitioned were unquestionable. Isolation from others did not exist. We had enduring friendships with many accepting folks who'd been privy to our unusual journey all along. There were the on-going connections to Niela—my friend, David's former therapist—and her groups. And we had a community of transgender friends whom we'd met at various events. With them, we'd been able to expose our difficulties regarding issues specific to transgenderism.

At Fantasia Fair each year in the fall, we'd attended multiple couple's workshops. I'd also gone to some that were just for spouses of Ts, led by Dr. Sandra Cole, a therapist from Michigan who specializes in transgender challenges. Sandra is a great champion of partners of Ts, as they deal with the unusual concerns associated with a transgender relationship. I'd found much comfort in her wisdom and guidance, as well as in the sharing with other wives and partners.

In other couple's workshops, David and I had explored more general relationship issues, making wonderful connections and finding common ground. We were invariably heartened in these settings, as we observed other couple's struggles and realized the exceptional degree of love, respect, and intimacy we have in our marriage.

As we traversed the transition period, I sought support and solace in every possible way: My summer escapes to the cabin and winters in the south, the caring of dear friends, a remarkable life coach, Janet Parker of Lifewise Trainings. I also had the on-going love and caring of a spiritual community in the Movement of Spiritual Inner Awareness (MSIA). At our monthly gatherings, I was always uplifted with encouragement and tenderness.

∞

As I neared my sixtieth birthday in May of 2009, months before we'd realized David's need to transition, I explored with Janet my feelings about reaching this ripe middle-age. I'd spent time defining and clarifying my life, recognizing the solid foundation of self-care I had established. It would serve me well in dealing with the unexpected, monumental changes ahead.

I made the observation that the source of my safety, even my happiness, lies within me. This was a liberating awareness. I had finally developed the self-care and respect that, to me, demonstrate God's love and light. I'd begun to see this energy as eternal and unwavering, with no question in my mind or heart that I was protected and guided.

I was on a sweet, satisfying path: Happily married, healthy, loving my psychotherapy practice with clients and couples, relishing the freedom of our empty nest. Approaching my seventh decade, I'd begun rejoicing in this stage of life, especially gratified by the accumulated wisdom and capabilities that had shown up. I knew that I had a solid foundation to uphold me, without even knowing what lay ahead.

Since fall of 2008, I'd been participating in a two-year Master of Spiritual Science program with Peace Theological Seminary. Through this work, I had formulated clear intentions for my life, including self-discipline, clarity, gentleness, and surrendering to God's peace. I was exploring the question, "What do I want to create in my sixties?" as a method for developing more intentions to guide me.

In the spring of 2009, I'd fashioned a positive affirmation for the decade ahead and beyond: *I am observing and trusting in all of life; seeking the underlying gifts in everything; loving myself, loving the process, and loving others.* Remarkably, I shared with my life coach, Janet, that I was actually looking forward to turning sixty. I welcomed continued opportunities for growth and introspection.

I was developing new levels of long-sought neutrality, building my ability to accept what I could not change, basking in the innate love I was experiencing, and finding less need for outside recognition. I'd become self-accepting, with a profound sense of peace, knowing that I am loved, regardless. I'd learned to look ahead to possible consequences before acting, to change course if I didn't like the outcome I foresaw. And I was content with my life, joyously telling Janet one day, "You know, I actually feel as though I'm becoming what God might intend for me to be!"

All of this self-awareness and trust had allowed me, had prompted me, to reach that spontaneous conclusion in September, 2009: That my beloved needed something other than one more antidepressant. Fortunately, I already recognized the inner foundation that would sustain me through the trials that followed.

∞

Alas—I was still human! Despite the recognition of my sterling spiritual qualities, I found it impossible to remain supportive and upbeat at all times (an absurd expectation, anyway). Stage Two of grief, Anger, began showing its surly face. I'd learned to be watchful of turning my anger inward, with depression the outcome. And there was plenty of disturbance that exploded outward.

I found it particularly aggravating, listening to David's recurring enthusiasm about bodily changes; his excitement for all that lay ahead. It annoyed and hurt me that his exhilaration sometimes seemed to render him unaware of the grief I felt. I'd sometimes lash out at him: "Oh my God, David! Can't you talk about anything else?"or "Do you have any idea what this is like for me?" Almost invariably, when I became distressed, sometimes getting pretty nasty, he understood how I was feeling and expressed compassion and regret for my difficulties with the transition.

His only "misdeed" had been accepting my encouragement to follow his lifelong dream and feel thrilled about it! How was I supposed to justify my anger at him? The feelings became displaced: I'd be short-tempered with the dog, annoyed at other drivers, bitchy about the weather, or my hair, or my clients. This seismic shift in our lives required hard work, and maintaining my equilibrium was a constant challenge. In the summer, I could hardly wait to get to the cabin, away from the constant reminder that my husband was morphing. I relied on that escape, my coaching with Janet, and all other known methods for soothing my soul and tempering my explosions.

In the eighties, I'd studied *A Course in Miracles,* channeled writings published by the Foundation for Inner Peace. I recalled the *Course* teaching that fear invariably underlies anger, and experienced and dealt with *both* emotions frequently. I attempted to list precisely what I feared (as if precision might help), knowing I was attempting to gain some sense of control in my life, my marriage, and the great unknown which lay ahead.

My fears were easily identified, rudimentary: Not knowing who we'd be as a couple after the transition. That we'd be seen as a lesbian couple. That we were freaks. That our marriage might not last. That we'd lose our family and friends. That the orthopedic practice might dissolve. That other jobs would not manifest for Deborah. To some extent, I feared *all* of the mysteries yet to be revealed.

One morning during my daily spiritual focus, I'd picked up a discourse containing the teachings of my spiritual guide, John-Roger. J-R is the founder of MSIA and the Insight Seminars, from which David and I had extracted so much value. His twelve years of discourses had been guiding me for some time. As is so often the case, I'd picked-up the perfect one to steer me toward a resolution for what was hounding me that day. It had helped to clarify the underlying choice I was making in support of the transition, and reminded me of a method for dealing with all of life's struggles.

J-R's words suggested that, if I desire something beautiful that I'm unable to obtain, I can simply decide to look in another direction. In so doing, I will see other things that I *can* have and begin moving toward them instead. By following this philosophy, I could achieve and maintain a positive focus, rather than allowing anger, resentment, and frustration to build over something unavailable.

I frequently applied this to my angst over David's transition and the wildly discomfiting thought, *I'm losing my husband.* I realized that, in turning-away from that thought, I was choosing to pursue a most precious relationship with my mate, albeit in a different form. While honoring my need to mourn the loss of my dreams and expectations regarding the *appearance* of our marriage, I was steadily progressing toward what I *could* have with Deborah. This definitely beat swimming upstream.

I had frequent phone coaching sessions with Janet and was immensely grateful for her support in dealing with my anger, as well as her ability to assist me in addressing the fears beneath it. We focused on what frightened me, then assessed the reality of my concerns and developed ways of dealing with them.

Janet often reminded me of a useful acronym for FEAR, from the Insight teachings: False (or Fantasized) Expectations Appearing Real. She suggested that *all* expectations set us up for anger and resentment if they're not met. This awareness assisted me in noticing that my anger invariably had expectations of some sort associated with it, and that fear was beneath it all.

A question from Janet once provoked my anger and a plethora of feelings to be addressed: "Leslie, with David now moving toward fulfilling his greatest dream, what's in this transition for you?"

At first, I'd been offended by this question; it seemed to imply that I should be selfishly looking for reciprocity for supporting my mate. But I'd had similar queries from several friends, and I knew the issue had to be addressed. The general concern was this: "Since David's getting exactly what he wants for his happiness and you're losing what you want, how can that be a good thing?"

I began to consider whether denial was still at work, despite thinking I'd unearthed and dealt with all of it. In encouraging David's transition, was I also loving and caring for myself? Was I honoring what I desired in my marriage? I had to pursue this.

Janet was aware that I, a social worker, sometimes had a tendency to "over-give," without attending to my own needs or even being aware of them. Years before, she'd been one of two facilitators in an advanced Insight training at which I'd expressed a frustration in my marriage—the recurring struggle to obtain what I desired sexually. These feelings had arisen when the men in the workshop had begun some sort of spontaneous male-bonding display. Dancing and gyrating together, they'd flaunted their masculinity and connection to each another.

The men's movements had been exciting to me on a primal level, and I'd been painfully aware that David would not have participated, had he been present in the training. Though he appeared to the world as extremely masculine, he simply had no innate sense of being a manly man; no desire to accentuate his maleness. I knew this sort of thing felt alien to him.

I spoke privately of my intense feelings with Janet and the other facilitator, both of whom knew David and were familiar with our transgender story. I bemoaned the absence of raw, male sexuality in my mate, simultaneously affirming my love and respect for him, my desire to support him in every possible way.

I was taken aback when one of them said to me, "Maybe it's time for you to decide what your role in David's life is going to be, Leslie. You're his wife, you know; not his social worker." That got me questioning whether I'd slipped into the role of therapist with my husband.

Later, I shared all of this with David and we both began to examine our marital roles. It had been grist for the mill of our growth and advancement, the kind of challenge that we know leads to more self-awareness, greater intimacy, and mutual understanding. It became clear that each of us plays a variety of roles in the other's life, depending on what's needed for us to maintain our loving, supportive relationship. And I'd realized it was time to ensure that I was truly caring for myself, as well as supporting and caring for my greatly-loved mate.

∞

During the two-year transitional period, I was encouraged by Janet to pay keen attention to my own wants and needs, while championing David on this journey. She repeatedly asked that critical question, "What's in this transition for you, Leslie?" I'd overcome my initial aversion and had begun to seek an answer. Eventually, I had a multi-faceted response:

By promoting the transition, I was supporting David in being wholly true to himself (or *herself*, his true identity). I'd been committed to being true to myself for many years, so I knew that encouraging David to do so ensured that I'd have a joyful, self-satisfied spouse. His (her) happiness could only increase my own.

There was continued intimacy of nearly every kind, now infused with David's joy, self-acceptance, and a reciprocal, unconditional love. This is why my anger never lasted for long. He invariably comprehended my frustration and pain, empathizing completely and gently comforting me.

106

Weekends together at our cabin had always been sweet, and they continued to be a favorite time to reconnect after a busy week. Our comfy chairs face the water, and we'd sit with our feet up, sipping morning coffee, sharing our exquisite view of Lake Winnipesaukee. Simply being there together as we read or caught-up with each other's lives felt special.

One morning a few months before the transition, I read aloud from a book I'd been enjoying, a compilation of love stories from "The Sun Magazine" called *The Mysterious Life of the Heart*. The title had seemed apropos to our situation. I'd chosen a narrative of an author's dilemma, shortly after his wife had died: He'd not known what to check for marital status on a form he was completing. It was a touching account of what he'd learned from her dying and death, and we were in tears by the time I'd finished reading. This had become a prelude to love-making, as the reading had resulted in both of us feeling so full of love and appreciation for each other, of our life together and what it would mean, to lose each other.

David's frustration and depression were evaporating. We'd had our challenges with sexual intimacy for two decades and had managed to overcome them, remaining committed and loving. With his newfound happiness, it became easier to address these issues more gently and kindly, even with humor. My being post-menopausal was a help, too; my libido had diminished considerably. I'd certainly never dreamed I'd come to appreciate this when it had begun, but I did now!

Since David had been on female hormones and a testosterone blocker, I had been on the receiving end of greater loving, acceptance, and flexibility than ever before. My mate no longer reacted with anger or withdrawal from me when minor incidents occurred that would previously have upset him. I'd await a typical irritated response and find it replaced by easy-going acceptance. Amazingly, he just stopped being annoyed.

I celebrated new levels of adherence to our Relationship Vision commitments, especially, "We are each other's best friend; We support each other's growth and healing; We are open to change; We share important decisions;" and "We create win-win solutions."

Since I'd become certain, by this time, that I would love and care for *myself—no matter what,* I was able to proceed with my support for the transition. Even without knowing its ultimate impact on our relationship, I anticipated staying married. I'd survived a divorce at thirty-two and knew I could handle that again, if necessary. Furthermore, I was reasonably certain that if our marriage ended, it would be handled with a great deal of tender, loving care.

With my high level of comfort with a cross-dressing husband, I felt at least somewhat prepared to handle the reactions from outside our marriage. I also expected many life-lessons ahead, something I always hope to welcome in my life, even the toughest ones. Ernest Hemingway said, "The world breaks everyone and afterward many are strong in the broken places." As a strong, resilient woman, I knew that I'd never be broken beyond repair.

I've said before that I could no longer watch my husband sink repeatedly into depression. It was simply too sorrowful for me to bear, now that we knew there was a logical, though difficult, remedy.

Finally, the bottom line was that *it just felt right to me,* perhaps in the same way David had ultimately known that it was right for him. This path would not lead to the ideal life I'd envisioned, but my visions of life had been morphing steadily for as long as I could remember. Depending on the decade, my ideal life would have included a walking mother, an adoring father, siblings who outlived our parents and were happy with their lives. I'd have had a first marriage that lasted a lifetime—and I'd certainly never have fallen in love with a married man in a dress!

Early in life, I'd detected that circumstances change life plans and I had learned to adapt. I knew that when a change feels right to me, I will alter my life plan and make room for a different ideal. If that doesn't work out, I start creating a new one. Long ago, without even knowing it, I'd embraced the Joseph Campbell philosophy on the plaque on our wall: *We must be willing to let go of the life we have planned so as to have the life that is waiting for us.* I was willing; I'd let go.

∞

CHAPTER SEVENTEEN
COMPLICATED JOURNEYS

JOURNAL ENTRY: D said this morning, "I've had another shift. Now I know for sure that this transition is going to happen." He seems to have reached a new level of self-acceptance and belief, both in his right to proceed and ability to allow it. He's excited.

Our situation is a Catch-22. He's told me many times, "I'll stop this if it means losing you." I could have told him to stop and it would have remained to be seen what transpired—misery and pain for <u>both</u> of us, I'm sure. I don't think he would ever have pushed forward if I'd said that. The distress would have continued and probably deepened. Maybe a suicide would have eventually ended it.

D is not one to say, "I'm doing this whether you like it or not." This is completely contrary to his nature and I'm grateful for that. But lately, I feel sad and agitated a lot. It's so damn hard going through this.

∞

DESPITE MY DESIRE FOR EASE and grace, this was not always the case. I struggled with the impending transition and changes along the way, sometimes finding it difficult to maintain my loving support and enthusiasm. David was filled with excitement about his bodily changes and the anticipated future as Deborah. Meanwhile, there was no question that I was grieving.

My husband's budding breasts did not excite me, nor was I pleased with myself in my reluctance to touch his chest. My lesbian sister had once kiddingly dubbed me a "hopeless heterosexual." Now, as my husband morphed, I again acknowledged the truth of that moniker.

Loving him the way I did and wanting to be totally accepting, I thought that I should overcome my resistance. But the honesty we both value compelled me to tell him of my unwillingness to touch him, and of my self-judgment that it seemed ridiculous to feel this way. We were sad about the situation, but accepted it as one more facet of this complicated transformation, both hoping it would eventually change.

Our affection continued with much of the snuggling and fondling we had always enjoyed. Through the years, we'd devised many ways of sharing sexual pleasure—with or without intercourse. This tenderness was maintained, despite my aversion to touching David's breasts and his own plummeting libido, a result of the medications he was taking.

When I wasn't sad about this, I was philosophical, perhaps rationalizing. I'd once heard the spiritual teacher Ram Dass speak of welcoming the diminishment of sexual desire. He'd asserted that, without it, there was much more energy, time, and focus for other things in life. Still, as someone who'd taken great pleasure in her sexuality, I grieved for my declining libido, now compounded by David's changes.

Naturally, I wondered whether he would someday want sex-reassignment surgery—removal of his penis and testicles, creation of female genitalia. This felt unacceptable to me. And he, overjoyed by my approval and encouragement, seemed to have all that he wanted. He'd never hated his genitals, as some transsexuals do, and believed that living as a woman would be enough. I felt pacified and pushed-away the concern. Yet, I was also mindful that he'd denied he was transsexual for many years, perhaps willing himself to be *just* a cross dresser. Time would tell; denial sometimes trickles away.

Pondering this was part of my process, of course. And I brooded over my hesitation to promote a complete transformation. It was I who had first suggested the transition. Why would I encourage his living as female, yet place such importance on the structure of his genitals? Simply put, I liked his penis. I liked being heterosexual. I hated the thought that he'd do away with this remaining vestige of maleness. Reluctant to touch breasts on my husband's chest, I feared a greater aversion to his having a vagina. I was aware that some part of me wanted to hold onto having a husband—*my* husband—despite my flexibility and lofty ideals.

He did investigate facial feminization, consulting a plastic surgeon who specializes in transforming the appearance of transsexuals from one gender to the other. We agreed that this surgery might be necessary for Deborah to appear more feminine, as David's face was decidedly masculine. What's more, he'd once broken his rather large nose and it had been crooked ever since.

Several factors put that idea on-hold. First was my adverse reaction to a film I'd watched, shortly after he'd begun hormones. The DVD, made by a transsexual friend, was about transitioning. When I saw the bandages following a facial feminization, I'd burst into tears. The man who'd transitioned was first shown as a handsome soldier in fatigues, with a big, cocky grin. Then he'd appeared with his (her) head almost completely swathed in gauze. Something about this sight pierced me deeply, painfully. I felt appalled at the prospect of my husband's doing this.

Surprised by my extreme reaction, I'd identified a link between the horror I had felt and the loss of my siblings to their violent, disfiguring deaths. I'd had a spontaneous aversion to someone with a perfectly good face having it surgically rearranged. Not very rational—but, then, what about *any* of this was? I felt irrational much of the time.

The surgical question for transsexuals, facial or genital, is controversial. Some outside the transgender sphere view it as a kind of mutilation. Yet those who want it, transsexuals who have it done, consider it correctional. I understood this; I was simply unable to overcome my initial horror.

Secondly, we noticed that the combination of gender-altering drugs had begun to soften David's face. This was creating a more feminine appearance and it seemed that surgery might not be necessary.

The third factor that negated facial feminization surgery was the brevity of David's time-off from work for transitioning. This amounted to just twelve days, for practical reasons. There was not enough time for surgery and recovery.

"Face-plucking" is what we eventually called the weekly sessions with the electrologist, for removal of David's beard. Most men would cringe at the thought of having this done, but male-to-female transsexuals generally believe it's essential. Women don't usually have beards. My husband was having every hair follicle on his face, neck, and chest zapped, then plucked. Many had to be done repeatedly; persistent whiskers often replace themselves.

Because the hair on his face was fair, the removal procedure was difficult. Darker, heavier hair is more easily detected and eliminated. He was consistently frustrated with the results of this painful, tedious procedure, since the diminishment of his beard was noticeable only to him. A small compensation was less frequent shaving. Fortunately, the fair hair on his arms and legs was diminishing, one effect of the medications.

I'd found it laughable when David said he doubted that his electrologist knew the reason he was having his beard removed. He hadn't told her, believing his secret to be safe, and I'd pointed out that men don't generally go through this procedure *unless* they're transgender. Then I had the opportunity to explore this with the electrologist herself.

We'd run into her at a church fair, several months after electrolysis began. David introduced us, then he and I resumed our wandering. He was elsewhere when I saw her again, and I couldn't resist asking whether she knew why my husband was having his beard eradicated.

"Of course I do," she said, "but I'd never let-on to a client unless he'd told me himself." This kind woman seemed to understand her clients' needs and used complete discretion, and I'd realized why David liked her so much.

This slow method of beard removal was augmented several times by trips to Texas for a more radical treatment. Each time he went, David spent two consecutive days on the table, his face anesthetized and a technician on each side of him, zapping and plucking. There were two three-hour sessions each day, with a one-hour break between them. It was brutal.

I was stunned by my first glimpse of my mate after his initial trip. I'd been in Los Angeles for a conference while he was in Dallas, so we'd met in Chicago for the same flight back to Boston. His face and neck were so swollen, distorted, and red, I practically wept when I saw him. He was in pain, looked freakish, and people in the airport were ogling him. It was startling to witness what my beloved chose to endure, to step into his true identity.

∞

Any doubts that David held were primarily connected to the continuity of our marriage, the responses of others, and the question of where the newly-emerged Deborah would be able to work. For months he had told me that he could hardly stand to wait any longer. It seemed that, once the decision to transition was made, containing the need to be Deborah was nearly impossible. "I want this to happen now!" he said repeatedly.

I was sometimes perplexed by the thought that this transition might not be the answer to my husband's longing for happiness. It seemed clear to him it was the ultimate solution. But he'd often spoken of his old deluded belief, that accomplishing some far-off objective would guarantee his contentment. Once he'd achieved his goal, however, he'd discover that whatever it was—the marriage, the medical degree, the children, the house, the surgical practice—none made him happy for long. He'd begin pursuit of another distant goal, again hoping for satisfaction. Despite his misguided thinking of the past, he was still convinced that transitioning was what he needed for the ultimate happiness. I'd just have to wait and see.

I reflected on my own experiences with happiness, what it meant to me. Sure, looking good made me happy. Some new thing that I'd wanted was briefly gratifying. Going fun places was exciting. In fact, many things made me happy in a *fleeting* way. But I believed in William Arthur Ward's declaration: *Happiness is an inside job*. I couldn't help being concerned by David's belief that dramatically altering his appearance and our lives would bring him lasting happiness. And what about its effect on others?

In one of my countless, wearying conversations about the transition, a friend who felt anxious for me and our families had speculated, "I just don't understand how he can do something that will hurt so many people!" My mate and I had considered this issue many times, discussing and questioning the concept of injuring others. This concern had been a primary factor in David's unhappiness, during all those years of hiding his true feelings; right up there next to the unrelenting shame.

I was aware that my friend's apprehension for me, and especially for our children, was a projection of her own feelings. Like many folks, she was incapable of imagining this strange circumstance without a sense of horror and fear. I knew I could be straightforward with her; she had been like a sister to me for decades and she'd known about the cross-dressing from the get-go. I'd actually told several close friends, back in 1987, about the amazing cross-dressed man I'd met at the Floating Circle.

When I'd heard her reservations, as I had from many others, I'd felt a need to justify David's choice, though I didn't like speaking for him in his absence. It added to my emotional turmoil and depleted my energy; and there was always the possibility that I was being inaccurate. Occasionally, for self-preservation, I'd simply tell people I could no longer discuss it. We had more than enough of our own challenges to resolve without needing to address the incessant concerns of others. Sometimes I just wanted to sink my head into the sand.

Most of the time, however, in spite of my weariness, I'd do my best to help people understand. We were both committed to educating others, and I knew we needed those devil's advocates. I gained clarity through responding to others' questions and observations.

Aiming for neutrality, I did my best to hear what was said, without reacting emotionally. I calmly assured our friends that David and I would keep doing whatever we could to ease the way for others. We were willing to explain, ad nauseum; to describe David's life-long struggle, clarify as best we could, then explain some more. We dealt with this question of hurting others repeatedly through the transition years, but here was the bottom line: This transition was not *against* anyone else. It was *for* David—and I was supporting it.

My mate and I had addressed this concept of "for me, not against you" many times in our marriage. We'd known that each of us would occasionally act in his or her own self-interest, despite the other's resulting objection or hurt. As kindly as possible, we'd explain, "I'm sorry if this is hurting you; it's not against you; it's *for me*.

For example, I made a decision early in our marriage that two-week vacations with my spouse and his children would no longer be a part of my summer plans. I'd endured several of these getaways with distressing results. My stepchildren (understandably, perhaps) had little interest in my presence on their vacations with Dad, and they were not particularly nice to me. And my husband focused so thoroughly on his children, he had little awareness of my presence.

One summer at the lake, I reached my limit. It was the year that the girls watered-down my shampoo and conditioner, and all the kids had unexpectedly blasted me with water balloons. Perhaps I was no good sport, but this was not a vacation for me!

I knew David would be irate if I left, but after much soul-searching, I had to depart for my own good. I explained to him that it was not against him or the kids, but for me. He'd been hurt and angry, as foreseen, and much painful processing had ensued. Yet, as with other disputes, this had eventually resulted in good learning for both of us, as well as the honoring of our agreement to be honest about our needs and to take care of ourselves.

∞

Whenever anyone implied that the transition was an infliction on others, David became angry and defensive. For decades, he'd taken care of others, putting most of his own desires on hold. He'd struggled through more than fifty years of shame, attempting to purge himself of this longing to be female.

At last he was taking care of himself. He'd begun to live his truth, and he was doing this with my blessing.

We did our damndest to clarify this for others, but many people failed to believe that the transition was anything but complete self-indulgence. We had to let this be *their* problem, not ours. The deepest longing of David's soul had dictated a course of action. And, while we wanted others to comprehend and accept, we would not allow their confusion and judgment to stand in the way.

A viewpoint of Nietzsche (this one's on the frige) works well for us: O*ne must still have chaos in oneself to be able to give birth to a dancing star.* We'd learned to live with chaos and trusted that this journey was worth enduring, whatever it entailed. Nietzsche's wisdom would have to extend to our withstanding the chaos in others, too!

I celebrated that my husband was finally saying, "If people have issues with this, those are their issues. They need to find a way to work through them. It's not up to me to deny my happiness so they can be comfortable."

Of course, losing our friends and family would be devastating if it occurred, and it was impossible not to fear this. But we had to trust that those who loved us would listen to our story, overcome their reservations, and love us enough to manage their own feelings about it.

Besides attempting to dispel concerns that the transition would hurt others, we dealt with the oft-asked question of why David needed *external* change to obtain *inner* happiness. One friend who'd been supportive of the transition from the beginning agreed that it's up to others to deal with their discomfort about it. But he was curious about the inner versus outer happiness question. "Here's what I don't get," he'd said to me. "I agree that we have to be true to ourselves. What I don't understand is why David needs to change himself on the outside, when what he wants to experience is really on the inside, isn't it?"

It was another of those times I wished that my mate had been present to reply for himself. I'd asked him the same question repeatedly through our years together, encouraging him to feel Deborah's presence within, regardless of how he was dressed.

But this had never been helpful or even doable. His best explanation had been that he needed to align the outside of his body with the inside, and he was finally convinced that he must make this change in order to be truly happy. I'd offered my best explanation to my friend, ultimately telling him he'd have to seek a more accurate response from David.

Later, I discussed the conversation with my spouse, and he'd responded with a query of his own. "So tell me, Sweetie—how come you couldn't be happy living in Nebraska?" Here was an ideal case-in-point; an experience from several years before which perfectly exemplified the inner-versus-outer happiness conundrum.

In 2003, David had vacationed with a friend on a dude ranch out west, returning with the idea of taking a job in Montana. By then, we'd remained in New England for years, to be near his children. But three of them were out of their mother's nest, and the youngest of the four was in high school. My husband was fed-up with practicing medicine in Massachusetts and was getting itchy feet. And I was delighted to entertain the possibility of an adventuresome move.

The position he looked at in Montana turned out to be undesirable, but he'd soon received a recruiter's letter for a job in the middle of the country. Seizing the opportunity, he joined an orthopedic practice in North Platte, Nebraska, "Gateway to the West." It wasn't Montana, but we were both game for the undertaking, filled with optimism and exciting plans. The move, in early 2004, had begun with a carefree six-week journey in an RV. I dubbed this our "Mid-life Midwest Adventure," and wrote about it daily on our trek.

Once in Nebraska, we'd purchased nearly 100 acres of land and started building our dream house. We bought horses (though neither of us had ever owned one before!) and began having incredible adventures on the backs of Annie Oakley and Gus.

The medical practice was outstanding. Since David had worked primarily in a specialized niche in Massachusetts, he was delighted to be using and sharpening all of his orthopedic skills in the new job. I obtained my Nebraska social work license, joined a private psychotherapy practice, and began to build a clientele.

In spite of it all, I was not happy in North Platte. My enthusiasm had started trickling-away after the first few months, when I'd begun to feel like a fish out of water, realizing I just didn't belong in the Great Plains. Naturally, I told David of my discontent, then I'd followed his sensible suggestion to call Janet Parker. Coaching had begun in earnest, with Janet listening reflectively to my griping. After hearing my description of the newness in our lives and how different this locale was, she had cried, "Oh my God, Leslie! I can see why you're struggling. You're having culture shock!" Her empathy was a balm.

Janet's assessment had been right. Nearly everything about our new life was foreign to me and I was struggling. Despite having wholeheartedly embraced this dream—building the house, becoming horse owners, moving two thousand miles across the country—I grew less and less willing to accept this novel life. I'd been taken aback by my unexpected change of mind and heart, and it was difficult to tell David that I was so distressed. But I couldn't keep this from my mate; my aversion to staying was overwhelming. I remember thinking that, if I'd had any doubts about our marriage, I might have told him, "I'm out of here! Do you want to come with me or not?"

I shared my distress, but affirmed that I'd carry-on for a while. David had a commitment to the hospital and I knew I could stay for a few years, as long as I had the option to call it quits at the end of that time. We both hoped that I would adjust, but this was not to be.

Eighteen months after the move—just six months into our new home—I'd had a major melt-down. This occurred after a short trip I took with a visiting friend from the east. We'd driven to Cheyenne, Wyoming, then down to Denver for another night. The next morning, my friend flew home and I attended a day-long social work training. The instructor was a Bostonian and I'd practically begged her to eat lunch with me, soaking-up that distinctive Massachusetts accent and imagining I was back in New England.

At the end of the day, I could barely force myself into the car for my four-hour drive back to North Platte, and the trip home was devastating. I wailed with homesickness, then I'd pull myself together, attempting to focus on my blessings. I lectured myself: "Get a grip, Leslie. Look what you have in your life: An adoring husband, a dream house, new friends, a great dog, your own horse, a growing psychotherapy practice, glowing health [yada, yada, yada]. Now shape-up!"

My tears would surge again, and I'd wonder whether to share this unhappiness with David one more time. I despised the thought of wrecking our new life and the dream we'd shared, but I knew it wouldn't be honest to try and hide it, and I needed to be true to myself. My outlook was definitely not improving; it was worsening by the day.

Arriving home, I revealed my increasing distress and, naturally, David had been upset. Within a couple of days, however, he'd told me that if I was *that* unhappy, we should go back east. Then he'd added that he wanted to leave as soon as possible, so he wouldn't be starting a new practice even later in his fifties. This was a total shock to me! I'd been willing to stay another eighteen months, at which point his commitment to the hospital would end. Moreover, we'd just moved into our gorgeous, custom-built home, and my practice was becoming established. I certainly couldn't discourage this new plan, though. My misery was the entire reason he'd so radically changed his thinking!

Within six months, we were back in New England. I couldn't help wondering how other husbands might have reacted to their wives' complaints, after so dramatic an undertaking. I'd felt grateful beyond words. My husband had understood and sacrificed for me—and I was back where I belonged.

Exploring with David the question of happiness that my friend had asked, I'd laughed in recognition when he'd brought-up our Nebraska fiasco. It was the perfect example of how I'd struggled to be happy, when external circumstances were throwing me into a tailspin.

In coaching, Janet and I discussed preferences—how we enhance our lives by the choices we make, thereby increasing our happiness. And I'd realized it was okay to be unhappy about something, despite having chosen and agreed-to it, and to make these feelings known to my spouse. I also saw the Nebraska experience as further evidence of how deeply David understands and appreciates me and my feelings; of what he's willing to do to rectify a situation that becomes objectionable to me.

To be true to ourselves and our deep longings whenever possible is a requirement in our lives, and we are committed to supporting each other in so-doing. Ultimately, it was this promise that led me to promote what he needed to do for his greatest happiness.

It is ridiculous to demand that others understand us, and know the truth about us. How is that possible? We can only do the best we can, in steady patience, and with inner reserves, knowing that we don't understand others, either. –Taylor Caldwell

∽

CHAPTER EIGHTEEN
TELLING THE FAMILY

JOURNAL ENTRY: Living this long seems to have brought more freedom, and I especially recognize and embrace greater levels of wisdom and experience. There's definitely less need to conform, less internal pressure to do anything I don't want to do. This stage of my life seems to be one of complete self-acceptance and a firmer definition of who I want to be, then being that; of clear choices regarding what I want to do; of needing less (or no) approval from others. It's definitely a freedom I've lacked in the past. I like it!

∽

I'D LONG KNOWN OF Christina Crawford's 1978 book, *Mommie Dearest,* depicting the alleged abuse by her famous mother, Joan. Christina's allegations had created long-lasting dispute and despair among family members and others. Though neither of our families had notoriety, I still wanted to avoid a similar scenario among us. So, I decided to give our relatives the opportunity to respond to anything I'd written about them.

Reactions had varied widely when we'd made our revelation, from complete support to estrangement. I knew that my account might differ from the way they'd seen and heard it. After telling our kids the news, we'd thought they had accepted it completely, so I was surprised when several asked that their names not be included in the book. I decided to be consistent and eliminate all of our children's names.

Then, after sending the rough draft of this chapter to our siblings to ensure that they'd be okay with it, I received some disappointing responses to what I'd written about telling them. It was painful to receive negative feedback from family members, but I was thankful I'd given them the opportunity. Negative reactions were unpleasant, but they simply reflected society's current position regarding transsexuality, and there's no getting around that. The Connecticut hospital debacle had demonstrated how narrow-minded and fearful people can be. We'd naively hoped that, with family, it might be different.

I rewrote the chapter, to be as gentle as possible with my treatment of the family. It had been foolish for us to think this would be easy for anyone. Early-on, we'd embraced John-Roger's wise counsel from Insight: *Hope for the best, prepare for the worst, and shoot down the middle.* Our dream of the best outcome was complete acceptance and support from our loved-ones. What we'd gotten was a mixed-bag.

Through the two transition years, we had fretted daily about whom, when, and how to tell—wondering, imagining, sometimes fearing the reactions we'd come up against. When the fall 2009 decision had been made for David to take hormones, we figured our first task was to tell our children. My two, and one of David's, were in their thirties; the three youngest were twenty-nine, -six, and -two. We'd actually told four of the kids about the cross-dressing in previous years, for a variety of reasons. Now that there would be a dramatic change, we needed to inform the two who hadn't been told at all, and the other four, plus a son-in-law, that there would soon be a major transition. We wanted to give them time to adjust, assuming they could even accept it.

∞

My daughter had been the first to know about the cross-dressing, even before David and I were married. She was in college, living in a Boston-area apartment, and had come to our western suburb for Thanksgiving, 1990. The event was going to be really special, the first family gathering in our new home.

We'd be joined by my in-laws, David's brother and sister, and their spouses and families.

My girl had arrived early, wearing jeans. Then she realized she'd forgotten her outfit for the holiday feast. I told her we'd find something for her to wear, and we headed for the bedroom closet. Looking through my clothes, she'd pulled out one of my dresses, wishing aloud that she could wear it, but she was a couple sizes larger than me.

Surprisingly, David happened to have an identical dress in a size that would fit this tall, young woman. He and I had seen it in a catalog and both loved it, and he'd surprised me by ordering it in both our sizes. I glanced at the matching dress, considering my daughter's possible reactions to my offering it, then grabbed it. I held it out to her, suggesting, "Here, try this on. I think it'll fit you."

"Oh, Mom! Did you get this for me? I love this dress!" she'd said excitedly. "Do you think it'll fit me?"

"No, I didn't buy it for you, but it might fit. Go ahead. Try it on."

"Mom—*are you pregnant*?" she'd asked with alarm.

"Oh God, no! Of course not! Besides, that's no maternity dress. Don't worry about it. Just put it on."

"Oh, well, David'll tell me when he gets back. Thanks, Mom!" she'd cried, and ran to get into the dress, which she'd worn for the rest of the day.

Since meeting David, I'd known that I'd be able to share the cross-dressing secret with my children, if ever the need arose. I'd raised them to be understanding, to accept differences, and they'd known of my sister's lesbianism. I wasn't overly concerned about the outcome of my offering Deborah's dress to my daughter, and she'd looked great in it.

David was on-call that Thanksgiving and had gone to see a patient at the hospital while we were dressing. Upon his return, I took him aside before he caught sight of her in the dress. The family had begun to arrive, so time was short. I quickly explained the sequence of events, reminding him of my children's open-mindedness, hoping he'd want to tell her that the dress was his.

Shortly thereafter, David came to me and muttered, "I've *got* to tell your daughter about the cross-dressing. I can't even look at her; I'm avoiding her. I don't want to go through the day like this." The old self-judgment had surfaced, but I reassured him about revealing his secret.

We sequestered my daughter in our bedroom, asking her to sit down for a minute. It was amusing that, despite being eighteen and a college student, she'd immediately thought she'd done something wrong. I was happy to tell her this was not about her.

She'd known about several cross-dressing parties we'd had; that we'd invited everyone to dress as the opposite sex. But she'd never suspected that David did this on a regular basis. Then the light had dawned when David told her, "That dress you're wearing—it's mine. I know it sounds weird, but sometimes I like to dress as a woman."

"Oh...really!" she'd replied, looking momentarily perplexed. "So that explains those parties you've had. Now I get it." And that was the extent of her reaction.

This daughter of mine loved and respected her future stepfather and had quickly accepted this minimal explanation. As if to demonstrate this, she'd returned for dinner a week later with gifts of makeup for Deborah, and I've never been prouder of my girl.

Next to be told was David's oldest child, a daughter who'd had surgery while in college. Coming out of the anesthesia, she'd revealed something intimate about herself to him, and he'd thought it would be encouraging to her, to know something confidential about himself. He said that he had something to tell her, just as she'd drifted back into her drugged haze.

Much to his amazement, she'd remembered. Several days later, she had asked him what he'd wanted to tell her. When he revealed that he sometimes liked to wear women's clothes, his daughter had been as accepting as mine, even disclosing that one of her friends dated a guy who sometimes did this, too. Another dent had been made in David's self-judgment, as he again realized what love and acceptance really mean.

At this point, we'd begun to realize that our children's generation was far more tolerant of divergent behaviors that we had been at their age. Two of our children now knew their father cross-dressed, yet it had seemed like a non-event in both cases.

Third to learn of David's proclivity, a couple of years into our marriage, was my son from the west, who'd come to New

England for a visit. When he'd arrived, we were unpacking the car from our week at Fantasia Fair, the annual transgender gathering on Cape Cod. He stopped his car just behind our SUV, where its wide-open back revealed a mound of women's clothes, a couple of wig boxes, and our make-up cases. My husband's continuing paranoia had surfaced immediately.

After we'd greeted my son, David anxiously whispered to me, "Now we have to tell him!" When I asked him why, he'd said, "I'm sure he's looked in the back of the car and he has to know all that stuff can't be yours. He must be wondering why we have so much female gear."

I'd been amused by his wariness and told him I doubted that my son had noticed anything unusual. Then I suggested that it might be a good time to tell him about the cross-dressing. David agreed, but—perhaps because of his persistent shame—he'd not opened-up to this male child of mine. He'd been slightly more comfortable telling our girls; apparently it was harder to reveal such a secret to the boys. David changed his clothes and slipped away to the office, leaving me to be the informant.

I actually welcomed the opportunity. It would feel good to me, having both of my children aware of something so important to David, so intrinsic to our lives together. My son and I took a walk, as I told him about his stepfather's odd proclivity. "David and I have just gotten back from a week on the Cape—and he wore women's clothes the whole time. It's something he really likes to do, and he's been doing it since long before we met. We've been at an event this past week that we go to every year, for transgender people and their partners."

"You mean he puts on everything that a woman would wear?" my son asked doubtfully. "Even panty hose?"

"Yep, even panty hose. He likes wearing women's things and he has for most of his life. Lots of those dresses in the car were his, and the boxes have wigs in them."

After describing the phenomenon as best I could and telling him that I support his stepfather in doing this, I'd encouraged my son to talk to David about it, to clarify things I couldn't explain. Then came his comical reply: "I can't believe he wants to wear all that stuff, Mom. It must be a pain in the ass to put it all on!"

We'd both been able to laugh about it, as my son just shook his head in astonishment.

So now, half of our children knew that their dad was a cross-dresser. We'd encouraged them to feel free to ask questions, but it appeared they wanted to know nothing more, at least not from us. Furthermore, all three had indicated they had no desire to see David en femme. He was out of the closet, but it seemed they'd just as soon have him remain there. We never pushed for more discussion. We trusted they'd bring it up if they wanted to know more.

The fourth of our kids to be told was the youngest, a little boy who kept asking about the wig in our closet. David had told him it was mine, that I sometimes wore it when I wasn't happy with my own hair; but he had persisted. He'd never seen me in the wig, so he wasn't buying that story, and he was fascinated by the hair on the shelf. We decided to take the most straightforward route; to tell him that the wig was actually David's, and briefly explain why his dad had a woman's wig. He was only about eight or nine, so our explanation had been a simple one: "Sometimes Dad likes to wear women's clothes," we'd told him. "There's nothing wrong with a man doing this, but not everybody thinks it's okay. In fact, some people get really angry about it, and even though we don't understand why, we're private about it and we don't discuss it with most people."

He'd seemed completely satisfied with this uncomplicated account and never brought it up again. It had appeared that his acceptance was as simple as our telling.

We've been asked why we hadn't told David's other two kids. It was simply that the need had not arisen, and because of their developmental stages. At times in children's lives, they have confusion enough about themselves, without throwing-in the disquieting information that a parent is transgender. Until the transition began, there had been no need to encumber these additional young lives with this knowledge. And we doubted that David's former wife had discussed this with the children. She'd been horrified with the knowledge and we thought it unlikely she'd mention it to them.

In 2009, the time had arrived when all of our offspring, then aged thirty-seven to twenty-three, needed to be informed that their father, my kids' stepfather, would be changing dramatically. We'd told my daughter and her husband about the transition on a visit with them in Florida. It had been good practice for telling the others and had probably been our easiest experience, as they'd been open to David's cross-dressing in their presence for some time.

They were surprised, but fairly comfortable and accepting of the transition plan. After some thought, our wise son-in-law had told me, "You know, Mom, at first I didn't understand why David would have to do this; but then it dawned on me that it didn't matter whether I understood or not. It's not about my understanding or anybody else's."

A decade before, this caring young man had won my daughter's heart and, while we'd never lacked evidence for understanding this, we now had an even greater appreciation for her amazing mate.

My son had lived with us for a year and a half during high school and cared deeply for his stepfather. Unfortunately, we'd had to tell him about the transition by phone, as he lived two thousand miles away and there were no plans to be together anytime soon.

His knowing since the mid-nineties that David liked wearing women's clothing had laid a foundation for some understanding, but he grappled with the new information. Shortly after our initial conversation, he'd called me and began to cry as we talked. It hadn't been long since his own dad had died, suddenly and unexpectedly. I doubted that my son had allowed himself to feel the depth of his grief. Now it appeared that his sorrow at losing his father was compounded by seeing David's transition as the loss of his stepdad. He said it seemed that he'd no longer have a father at all.

I'd automatically slid into therapist-mode with my son. He needed to be heard and have his feelings acknowledged, which I did for some time. He also needed reassurance that David was not technically going away; that he'd just be in another form. "Of course Deborah will want to do the things that David's always done," I'd assured him. "She'll be there for you in all the same ways."

Eventually, despite my efforts at gentle counsel, my own sadness and sense of loss began to surface. I was so tired of dealing with the entire issue that I ran out of steam. In a true therapy session, of course, I'd have recognized my reaction as what therapists call countertransference, an emotional reaction to a client's issues. I'd have set aside my own feelings until I could deal with them after the session. But this was my son; I was not his therapist and he was no longer a little boy. I had needed to disengage from his sadness and my efforts to address his feelings, as I wrestled with my own upset. I was no longer in therapist *or* mothering-mode.

"I think you miss your father more than you realize," I told him. "It's probably good for you to have all these feelings; they're to be expected. And I'm sorry you're having such a hard time, but I just can't talk about it anymore." I'd ended the call.

The following day, after processing this with David and having a good night's sleep, I reverted to my favorite method of sorting my feelings and regaining a healthy perspective: Writing. I cranked out an e-mail to my son, hoping to provide guidance and support for his difficulty and offer additional perspectives:

My dear son,

I know this is difficult and challenging, and it will take time for you to adjust. It would be unreasonable and unrealistic to expect you kids to accept this immediately or without a struggle. In David, you've experienced a solid, loving father-son relationship. Now that man is becoming something different, but the love won't go away. Deborah will be the same kind, caring person David has always been. The biggest change will be the happiness that he will finally experience, after decades of deep sadness and longing.

You are accurate in calling the transition selfish, but I hope you can understand that this choice is more about David's self-preservation and contentment than about being selfish. He's been ashamed of the transgenderism for most of his life and has actually been close to killing himself because of it.

After all David's years of giving and caring for others, of denying his true self and pushing down his own feelings and desires, don't you think it's time for my sweet husband to have what he's always wanted? Do you think it would be fair to ask him to deny his deepest longing to take care of you guys and your feelings? I don't think so. You kids are supposed to be grown up now.

We have no intention of hurting anyone, my son, and the thought of losing any of you is devastating. But it's up to each of you to determine how to deal with this. We can only hope that those whom we love will continue to love us and maybe even want to deepen the relationships. Time will tell.

Please consider talking with David sometime soon, 'cause I can only give you my thoughts and impressions. It's up to him to do some of the explaining to you and the rest of the gang. We will both assist you as much as possible and answer all of your questions to the best of our ability.

Dearest love always, your mom

PS I hope that you will one day know the kind of love that David and I have, my son. Each of us is greatly concerned about the happiness and well-being of the other, and we have an honesty that is rare. David has said many times that he will stop this transition if it means losing me. My reply is that I do not come with a guarantee (none of us does, in fact). But for me to deny him his greatest need in order to keep me is not the kind of marriage that I want. I have also told him all along that I do not know what this will mean for us in the long run. How can I possibly know?

I did not receive a response right away, but I'd given him a lot to think about. I guessed that he was upset with me for having ended our call abruptly, essentially telling him, "This is what's happening; I'm sorry if you have a problem with it." David and I had often joked about my perverse temptation to use what we'd dubbed "smack therapy" when clients resisted seeing reality and finding ways of dealing with it. In a way, I had done this with this my son. Now I needed to trust that he'd work through his issues and find healthy ways of grieving his own father's death and the transformation of his stepfather.

It took some badgering to get David to proceed with telling his own kids. His life-long shame, coupled with fear of hurting his children and of how they might respond, made him reluctant. There was also the geographic challenge. While we wanted the revelation to be made in person, if possible, two of his kids lived in distant states, and a third would soon be moving west. So, David took this youngest son hiking, a good venue for a father-son talk. This was the one who had asked about the wig, so he'd known of his dad's cross-dressing for more than a decade.

Naturally, he was shocked by the new information. Questions like my son's came forth, especially whether Deborah would still like to do the things they'd always done together. David assured him that becoming Deborah would not alter his enjoyment of everything he'd always liked to do.

Beyond expressing his concerns about how much things would change in their relationship, this 23-year-old seemed ready to accept the transition of his father, though he made it clear he had no desire to see his dad en femme anytime soon. His up-coming move out west would make it simple to avoid this. Furthermore, since the transition had just begun, we'd had no idea when it would be complete.

David's second daughter, one of the two kids we hadn't told about the cross-dressing, lived on the west coast. We decided to go there for Thanksgiving of 2009, so he could tell her. Meanwhile, I pestered him to make a date to tell his older son, the only one remaining in the Boston-area. I thought he should have the news before we left for our holiday.

It was easy to make an arrangement, and they'd met near-by for dinner. Though he'd not revealed that he cross-dressed to this son, David was surprised to learn that he already knew about it.

130

He'd been told by his younger brother some time before. This eased the way for David to inform him that he was transitioning, and this son also seemed to accept with minimal reaction. His primary concern appeared to be the desire for David to stay away from his friends after he transitioned. He was also uncertain when he'd be ready to meet his dad in the feminine mode; but he'd seemed okay with it, overall.

The west coast daughter was excited about our visit, as we hadn't seen her in some time. We'd flown out on Thanksgiving Day and gone directly to a restaurant for dinner, not the time to tell. David wanted a quiet twosome with his daughter for the revelation, and they'd gone to breakfast the next morning. As he'd explained what was happening in his life, he discovered that she, too, had been informed of the cross-dressing by her younger brother some time before. Obviously, there'd long been discussion among David's kids. This daughter was calm and accepting of the latest development; it seemed not to be an issue for her.

Later, as David and I explored her reaction, we'd recognized that all six of our kids had known about the cross-dressing for years. We were sad that none had ever raised the issue with us. We'd have clarified and explained it as best we could, if we'd had the chance. There could have been open dialogue about transgenderism, and we might have been reassuring our children and answering their questions all along.

We surmised that, after learning that their father cross-dressed, it had been an embarrassment to them and they'd wanted nothing more to do with it. Furthermore, David's immense shame had deterred him from ever bringing it up with them again, after the initial disclosure. There was just no negating the discomfort most people felt with the topic; and David was their dad, not some anonymous talk-show guest. Instead of candid discussion through the years, we'd reached this point of needing to reintroduce the subject, to inform them that David was morphing into a full-time woman.

Upon our return to the east coast, there was e-mail feedback from the west coast daughter. As with my son, she seemed to take issue with the selfishness of David's choice, perhaps not grasping the enormity of his life-long angst. She'd expressed apprehension for herself and her siblings concerning his appearance on their wedding days, though none was planning to be married any time soon, as far as we knew. She had written that she thought the happiness of the bride or groom should supersede David's happiness; that he ought to be prepared to resume the role of a father for these events. In a later e-mail, she'd kindly expressed concern that she might have hurt her dad's feelings.

Planning responses to her e-mails had led to more deep discussion for the two of us. We wanted to make this as easy as possible for our children, yet there was no denying or side-stepping their uneasiness. Perhaps this daughter needed more information about David's history and the agony he'd suffered. He'd also need to stand firm in his resolve to continue transitioning. He wrote her:

Hi, Sweetie.

No, you did not hurt my feelings. Believe me, everything that anyone can say to me has already been said, and I've said it all to myself, too. I've tried to resist this for nearly sixty years, and now I need to be at peace with it.

I care so much about you kids; your needs and wishes are important to me. But what I wear to anyone's wedding is not a concern right now. Don't worry; I'm not about to do anything crazy or hurtful! I think I've been a good parent, hanging-in there with all of you guys through lots of crap. Can you do that for me, too? I need for you to meet me half-way.

Here are a few things that I said in a church service that Leslie and I did. They're things I want you to know about me: "There is one thing that transsexuality is not: It is not a choice. I did not choose this. ...No one would have voluntarily chosen the pain this has caused me. My only choice now is whether to accept myself and live in happiness, or continue to live in hiding and shame.

...Not a day has gone by that I haven't thought I'd rather be a woman than a man. ...I have stumbled my way to this point in my life and now wish to bring my outer self into harmony with my

inner spirit. ...The pain that this may cause will be far less than what I'd experience if I don't take this path."

I know this sounds melodramatic, but it's not. I hope it will help you comprehend. Please understand that I cannot stop my progression on this path; it would be much too painful now. Let's all continue to be open with each other about our lives. I'll never stop loving any of you and I hope that you can all say the same of me. Thank you for supporting me.

I love you. Dad

We felt relieved at this point; both of my children knew and three of David's had been informed. No one had exploded, disowned us, or dissolved at the news. David's older daughter, who'd been so accepting of the cross-dressing years before, was the last to be told, simply because of timing and geographical location. We were hopeful that she would continue to be open-minded and understanding.

Early in 2010, David had flown to her city to reveal the transition plan. Once again, his disclosure was met with a positive reception, as we'd hoped. Gaining this reaction from the sixth child (plus our son-in-law) felt liberating. It had spurred David on in his quest for femininity.

∞

Once the kids had been informed, we began to consider how to tell other family members. I was agitated about explaining the transition to my brother, the only remaining member of my family-of-origin. I feared his rejection since he'd not been understanding of our sister's lifestyle, after she'd come-out as a lesbian. I doubted that his attitude had altered much in the two decades since her death; and, if this were true, I wondered whether his mind-set would extend to transgender folks, as well.

He had seemed a kinder man as he'd aged, more understanding of life's permutations. I'd attributed this to the aftermath of our younger brother's death in 1973. It seemed to me that suicide had caused our remaining family members to find better ways of loving and accepting one another. Still, there was the painful memory of his disapproval of our sister.

My brother had loved and admired David, finding much in common with him during our twenty-year marriage. They were both pilots; had enjoyed sharing their stories of flying. Each had a military background and was a scuba diver. There'd been reason to hope that he would remain in our camp. By summer of 2010, I needed to take some action to relieve my apprehension.

I had often locked horns with my brother throughout our lives, with his wife of forty years providing a gentle buffer between us. She had also loved our sister, accepting her lifestyle without judgment. So David and I had felt comfortable revealing the cross-dressing secret to her on a visit in 2004. She'd told us that she was honored to be trusted with the information, but reiterated a warning my mother had issued years before: "I don't think you should tell your brother about this; I doubt that he'd be very accepting."

We'd heeded this advice until now, but the warnings to avoid telling him were feeding my angst. Deborah would emerge within a year or so, and I was tired of fearing my brother's reaction. After much angst and discussion as we attempted to formulate a plan for revelation, I told my sister-in-law what was in the works. As expected, she was incredibly positive regarding the new development, and David, she, and I had begun a three-way conversation, through phone calls and e-mails, since they lived on the opposite coast.

She mulled it over, then suggested that she be the one to reveal the transition news to my brother, explaining that he'd sometimes regretted angry words, spoken in haste, that he couldn't retract. If he responded harshly when she was our messenger, he'd have time to cool-off before we spoke with him, and we'd not be the recipients of an impulsive reaction. This offer brought me great relief. It made perfect sense and let us off the hook—for the time-being, anyway. We sent our sister-in-law copies of *True Selves* and *She's Not There* to enhance her understanding.

By November, she'd felt ready for the task. She said that she, too, was afraid of my brother's reaction and expressed regret that we'd had this fear hanging over our heads. She was anxious to relieve us of this concern. David responded to her in an e-mail:

My first reaction to your offer was to fall back into the old shame and denial I've felt for almost sixty years. Why should I put other people through this when I can just keep it to myself? Well, as you know, hiding this has brought me only pain and depression.

I'm profoundly sorry for whatever grief this will cause others, but I've glimpsed the happiness of being true to myself and I must choose this path. I'm happy and I like the feeling; it's a new experience for me. Leslie and I both appreciate your understanding and willingness to support us, and we're ready for you to proceed. I've been blessed by Leslie's love; and now, by your loving support, as well.

Our sister-in-law had replied, expressing her gratitude for feeling closer to my mate than ever before. She said that she'd never known David very well and added, "I feel that I'm getting to know you for the first time. And I'm in awe of your courage!"

Not long after these exchanges, we heard from her again, saying that she'd told my brother and felt "pleasantly surprised by his reaction." She wrote:

He was initially stunned, almost disbelieving. He just sat for a long time, letting it settle-in. He finally said, simply, "Poor David." He has empathy for the life you have lived and the difficulty inherent in making your decision to live as Deborah. He added that he didn't think anyone should have to live a lie.

She concluded by telling us that my brother was uncertain whether he'd be able to feel comfortable with Deborah. She also said that she'd told their sons and their spouses on Thanksgiving. I was again struck by the flexibility of that younger generation; both couples have transgender and gay friends, and it was not an issue for them.

We were thrilled and relieved to know that my brother had been informed and that his reaction was nothing like what we had imagined. His wife was hopeful of his eventual acceptance, and we wondered whether it might be possible for the love to continue unabated. After decades of shame and hiding, David was amazed at the acceptance and kindness that was coming-forth. He replied to her e-mail:

Don't worry about not understanding this situation. No one, even Leslie and I, really understands. It's enough that her brother is willing to listen and care. As you know, I've been ashamed of myself for most of my life. It has taken so much energy to keep myself closeted, and now that I don't need to hide, I feel incredibly free. The real me is becoming acceptable to myself and others, and I'm happier than I ever believed possible. I find that I have more of myself to share with Leslie. It's truly amazing!

When David heard from my brother, we were at first elated; then the rain began to fall on our parade. He wrote:

My affection for you is unchanged, and I admire and respect your strength and tenacity. I feel empathy for the pain you've endured for so many years. You have a beautiful spirit. You've given so much in service to the human race on a variety of levels, and you've done this while bearing the pain of an existence you must now embrace.

I must tell you, however, that I face a dichotomy: Despite loving you as a brother, my nature does not allow me to embrace you as the married, female mate of my sister. This will have to be resolved in my psyche and I don't know how long that will take. I'm glad that you can find happiness in life and I admire your courage. I bless your happiness, but I don't know whether I can share it with you.

I love my brother David.

We were shocked. It seemed to us that my brother had supported my mate, but was rejecting us for the desire to remain in our marriage. David was angry, and I was alternately enraged and devastated. I could hardly believe that my closest remaining family member might reject us, simply because of my choice to continue our relationship. It remained to be seen, of course, what would transpire after my brother had taken his indeterminate time to "resolve this in his psyche." Well, at least the ball was now in play.

We had heard it said that a transsexual who chooses to transition must be prepared to deal with losing *everything*: spouse, children, family, job, income, home. While we'd not had losses thus far, this was beginning to look like our first. David e-mailed my brother:

You know, I'm prepared to lose friends and family because of this, but I hope you're not among them. I'd like the bond between us to continue. I'm still the same person you have always known—just a lot happier now.

Whatever you decide, though, please don't cut your sister out of your life. She has cherished the closeness you two have had and I don't want to see her hurt. I've told my own brother about the transition and it seems that he and my sister-in-law no longer wish to be around us. I have no idea what my parents will have to say when we tell them.

Since we live three thousand miles apart, it shouldn't be difficult to avoid seeing each other, but I hope that will not be the case.

For several weeks, e-mails were shared among the four of us, as my brother attempted to work-through this revelation of ours. Our sister-in-law was endeavoring to encourage his acceptance and asked that we be patient with him, saying that he had become "a person who is willing to contemplate a situation that he can't ignore."

In an effort to explain our stance I wrote:

I want you to know that David and I feel the same way about this transition. Our happiness precludes accommodating others' judgments, discomfort, and pain. We care about you and love you, but this transition needs to proceed, regardless.

I do sometimes feel that I'm losing my husband. In a way, I am. I've told David many times that I don't know what will happen with us down the road, because I'm always as honest as I can be, and I've never held such a challenging combination of paradoxical feelings. But one thing I do know is that my desire for my mate's happiness, a happiness that goes way beyond the physical, is what I want for him (soon to be her).

My brother responded:

My discomfort is not for David's scenario; I'm perfectly happy for him to be a woman. It is his spirit for which I have developed my affection. Where I'm out of my comfort zone is with my sister entering into a gay marriage. This is an area of extreme discomfort to me; it's one which I continue to oppose mentally, if not practically. I view marriage as an institution that is blessed for the biological reason of procreating the human race. Nonetheless, I love you—and I guess that defines the end.

I was working hard to understand my brother's stance and be as gentle as possible, though I could hardly bear to think there'd be conditions on his love for me. Yes, this would be a huge lifestyle change for us (though not for him). But how could he speak of my "entering into a gay marriage" when we'd been married for two decades? I tried to remain calm and wrote him back, explaining my philosophy:

I get how challenging this is for you. Believe me, it's far from easy or smooth for either of us. But here's something for you to think about: I have no desire to be married to a biological woman. I'm heterosexual. In loving this person/soul, now a man named David, in supporting him in becoming who he truly is, do you think that the transition makes my love go away? Or that I should selfishly demand that he deny what he longs to become, just to stay married and be considered a heterosexual couple? This is ludicrous to me. You say that I'm "entering a gay marriage," but this individual has been my spouse for twenty years! As for becoming a lesbian couple, I suppose the world may view us in this way. But we know who and what we are, and so do you. Who cares what anyone else thinks?

We eventually ran out of things to say, feeling frustrated and sad that my brother was not ready to accept. Perhaps this would change with time. We would give him the space he needed, hoping that the love we'd shared would surmount his prejudices. His wife wrapped it up with a kind message to David:

Your happiness, wholeness, and the emergence of real feelings are the important things. With great joy, I imagine how wonderful it will be when the whole transition process is complete and you can live fully and openly as yourself. I send much love and endless admiration.

∞

David's own brother had been told early-on, and he'd been far more decisive than mine. He'd made it perfectly clear that he and his wife would maintain a relationship with us only insofar as family events required. He'd also indicated that their adult daughters and husbands felt the same way. Our family appeared to be shrinking.

When we'd told David's sister, however, we'd gotten the best we had hoped for, as with my brother's wife. Not only had she been completely understanding and supportive, she'd wept for her brother's lifetime of sadness and shame. She also said she had always wanted a sister, so some of the tears were for lost years of growing-up as the only girl in their family. Since our revelation, she's been completely accepting and delighted to have Deborah as a sister. She's welcomed her with open arms—a true blessing.

∞

The only close family who remained uninformed were my in-laws, both in their nineties. We kept hoping for a way to avoid telling them, believing it would be too difficult to explain; possibly a cruel infliction on such elderly folks. After-all, this was their *son* of sixty-plus years. We were fairly certain they'd never imagined he was anything other than one of their two male offspring.

Our decision on this final piece of family business was to do nothing at first, hoping that an answer would emerge. We would wait and see what transpired after the transition.

The way to get started is to quit talking and begin doing. –Walt Disney

∞

CHAPTER NINETEEN
PICKING THE DATE

JOURNAL ENTRY: I guess we're staying in Gardner, for awhile anyway. So much is going on! We're going to go ahead and sell the house, even after all of our remodeling and expense, and move to a rented condo. And, oh yeah, my husband will soon be a woman. We have no idea how this will go at the hospital, assuming we do stay. Such adventures we're having (at least I'm <u>trying</u> to see it that way). Most couples our age are thinking about the adventure of retirement, but it seems that's just far too tame for us!

∞

BY EARLY 2011, WE KNEW for sure that the transition was going to happen and began to consider David's next steps to becoming Deborah, full-time. The jobs he'd checked-out had not manifested, so it looked like we had no choice but to remain where we were and see what transpired. Though we'd not yet determined exactly when the transition would take place, figuring out how to go about it had now become imperative to him.

Road trips are always good opportunities to discuss things, and we'd taken advantage of a winter trek to Vermont to determine what tasks lay ahead. Thinking in terms of a long list, I'd brought a pad of paper to record our thoughts as we organized them. Our dissimilar styles had rapidly emerged as David specified his goals for becoming Deborah: "Well, if I have facial feminization surgery, I'll only need about a week or so for that. I've got to get my hair at the Hair Club. And I want to have my ears pierced and my nails done. That's about it, I think."

"Oh, my God, Honey! Are you crazy?" I'd retorted. "There is *so* much more than that!" (I'm the detail half of this couple and was often the practical one, when it came to this enormous, life-changing event.)

"We need to write letters to our friends and extended family. You'll have to write another one for your colleagues and one for your patients, too. And you'll need to tell the dentist and any doctors you see, won't you?"

"What about telling your office staff, the medical staff, and the hospital board, too," I'd continued. "Think about all the documents that will need changing—your driver's license, for starters. In fact, how do you plan to go about that?"

The discussion had resumed and, ultimately, my reality check had led to the following list:

> - facial feminization surgery (with one week+ to recover)
> - hair enhancement
> - acrylic nails
> - ears pierced
> - expanding Deborah's wardrobe
> - name and gender change: Social Security card, driver's license, medical licenses, credit cards, insurance policies, passport, diplomas, legal documents, etc.
> - informing remaining family members and friends, office staff, colleagues, the hospital board, patients, service people, such as the dentist, etc.

Our mobile discussion determined no date for the transition, but at least now there was an agenda to follow.

Throughout the year, discussions of the impending change grew more lengthy and frequent, and David's need to become Deborah intensified. As we revealed the plan to more and more people, our lives became an open forum for speculation. We were creating this flurry of advice and copious opinions by informing others; but, while David never tired of it, I found it painful and exhausting.

Through everything ran threads of my concern and doubt, not that I would stop loving my mate or even that I'd want to leave. In fact, when David had first expressed the fear of losing me, I'd made a promise: "I will *always* love you, Sweetie—regardless. If I decide I can't stay, I promise to be your best friend." It had been the most I could offer regarding our future together. There was no question that I'd support the transition and continue to care deeply for this dear person, even if I found I couldn't remain in our marriage.

I had only my imagination to guide me on this, but I made a concerted effort not to let it run wild. My fear was sometimes palpable, but I managed to address it, to keep it at bay, bearing in mind that each concern was a fantasy which might never come true. With my life coach and friends, I worked-through whatever came up; and I discussed every disquieting notion with David, receiving incredible tenderness and support.

A mixed-bag of feelings and thoughts persisted on a daily basis. So many things—images, words, actions—triggered changes of emotion, of mind, of heart. Sometimes I reached a point of simply shutting-down. My tolerance for ambiguity remained intact, but my tolerance for *talking* about it all, and for the intense focus on the transition and the unknowns that lay ahead, sometimes just ran out.

As the gender change became imminent, my attention to David's appearance increased. My concern went beyond whether he needed a haircut or had a spot on his shirt and should change it before leaving for work. One of the nurses at the hospital had noticed something around his eyes and asked one of the physicians whether Dr. Fabian was sick. This, coupled with the facial-softening effects of the hormones, had given rise to concerns for David's health. After that, I'd begun checking carefully for remaining hints of eye shadow from the night before, imagining how obvious any little smudge would be above a surgical mask.

My heightened observations were also the result of a new realization: That probably within the next year, I'd no longer have the luxury of seeing this man—my beloved David—walk out the door. This reality repeatedly stunned me and was painful

143

beyond words. I wondered whether it was akin to knowing one's spouse is dying. As I'd pondered the analogy, I was acutely aware that there would still be a body, albeit changed, and a soul to continue loving. I was grateful for this; but how could I help but wonder, with trepidation, how the changes would alter our lives?

At this point, I probably came closest to the depression that's predicted in the stages of grieving. I was, at times, mired in sadness and loss. Ironically, it was I who continued to tell my grown children, "David's not going away. The form will be changed, but the essence of this man will always be there." Did I believe this myself? Intellectually, I did; and I *wanted* to believe it. But I knew that I'd miss the maleness that I'd known and loved; that persona which David had always resumed, after venturing out as Deborah.

There'd been no denying my desire to remain wedded to the man that I'd married twenty years before; but here's where love, for me, is defined by the range of acceptance it encompasses. I know it's a subjective matter, what one can accept in another, in the name of a loving commitment. For me, for now, I'd "stand by my man," as ludicrous as that statement sounded!

Naturally, I wasn't sad all the time; sometimes I was livid! I suppose this was my version of anger, from the stages of grief. It resulted from what I saw as foolish choices my husband began to make, as the stifling of Deborah, so close to a full-time life, had become almost unbearable. With the certainty of transitioning, he'd become more daring.

One evening in the summer of 2011, I'd opted to remain at our New Hampshire cabin, rather than return to Massachusetts for a wine-tasting dinner at a restaurant, with friends. I'd been unaware that my spouse had decided to go as Deborah until she called me from the road, on her way to the event.

I was appalled to discover that David had dressed. I knew that one couple in the group, another physician and his wife, had no prior knowledge of Deborah's existence. When I asked her about this, she'd casually said, "Oh, I told him at the hospital today; he's fine with it. He said he'd tell his wife, and he was sure that she would be, too."

This had seemed incredibly inconsiderate and unfair to me. I thought of the man's wife; of the awkwardness of these two attempting to grasp the revelation, then going to dinner with Deborah, perhaps in extreme discomfort.

I'd also thought that the proximity of this restaurant to the hospital and our hometown meant that other diners might recognize David—in drag. I expressed my concern and Deborah told me with nonchalance, "Oh, I'll just turn around and walk out if I see someone who might know me."

"And what if you're already seated and people walk in who recognize you?" I'd squawked.

For some reason, no concern was reflected back to me. I was enraged at what I saw as extreme lack of caution; careless, short-sighted actions, resulting from my husband's intensifying desire to live as Deborah. My mate's growing enthusiasm and positive experiences with a select group of supporters had lulled her into being exceedingly unguarded.

Another incident that summer had me reverting to an old, incredibly immature behavior: I ran away. Our summer haven, a hundred miles from home, makes for a great escape. Since we'd bought it in 1998, David had encouraged me to enjoy it as much as possible, whether or not he was free to go; but I doubt that he was thinking of my indulging an infantile impulse to bolt away from him when the going got tough!

Recall, here, that I'm a couples' therapist, though (obviously) not always practicing what I preach. I remind you that therapists are human, too. It was one of those times that I simply could not handle further dissection of the issues-at-hand. I wasn't proud of leaving in an angry state; of jumping in my car and taking-off with no explanation, other than my wrath. But I'd had to get away.

I'd been upset by the absurdity of a phone call we'd had, as I was returning from the cabin. I'd wanted to be with David, since he was on-call in Gardner that weekend; but during the conversation, we'd gone from selling our house and moving, to not selling or moving, yet continuing to search for a condo, as if we were moving. Then, when I arrived home, he'd immediately left to care for a patient. I'm sure this triggered my old

145

abandonment issues, piggy-backing on the disturbance and confusion I was already feeling. I'd given-in to my need to flee; jumped back in the car and returned to the cabin.

Fortunately, the two-and-a-half hour drive provided a cool-down period and a return to rationality. I reviewed our current life: We were in the midst of deciding whether to sell our home of five years, after the Connecticut hospital had promised a job, then retracted it. We'd experienced discrimination and were fearful of its happening again. David had investigated at least twenty orthopedic jobs and been turned-down by each, primarily because of his honesty and openness. We would probably give up our house (which we loved), *if* we could find a suitable alternative in which to live. The transition would be happening soon and we had no idea how the community would respond. And, oh yeah; I'd soon no longer have a husband. The enormous uncertainty, the drastic change in our lives—it had all been too much for me that day.

Gradually recalling my commitment to self-compassion and forgiveness, I cut myself some slack. I'd realized that fleeing is sometimes preferable to fighting, knowing with certainty that I'd been ready to do one or the other. By that evening, I was able to speak civilly to my beloved, finding him compassionate and forgiving, as well. And we'd worked through it all and returned to our loving by bedtime, able to wish each other a good night.

At some point during the summer of 2011, a solid plan materialized. Since a job had not manifested elsewhere and there was a growing constellation of encouraging supporters at the hospital, we determined that remaining here was our most viable option. We concluded that renting would be wiser than owning, should things not go well in Gardner; found a near-by place to rent, proceeded with the sale of our house, and moved.

Oddly, it was David's position on the hospital ethics committee that led to deciding when Deborah would appear full-time. Tasked with providing topics and speakers twice yearly for grand rounds (weekly presentations to the medical staff for their continuing education), he decided to use one of these presentations to introduce the new woman to his colleagues. He'd excitedly told me, "You know, transgenderism and the way Ts are treated by medical personnel are definitely ethics issues. So, I've decided to use the October meeting to come-out at the hospital and present *myself* as the topic!"

"Well, why not?" I'd replied. "It's an opportunity; may as well put it to good use. And you'll definitely have a captive audience."

Now we knew when David would cease to exist, and it had felt good to put an end to at least some of the ambiguity. We began planning for the fall and a whole new life.

PART THREE
A NEW WOMAN APPEARS

October 2011

AUTHOR'S NOTE

Part Three describes the first year following Deborah's transition: October 2011 to October 2012, our first twelve months in a radical, new life. It was a highly challenging time. My journal entries from this time period seem best to express how this difficult year transpired. What follows is a larger look into the privacy of my journals, unfettered by narrative.

Write what should not be forgotten. –Isabel Allende

∞

CHAPTER TWENTY
DAVID IS NO MORE

10/12/11: LAST NIGHT WAS our final dinner as the couple we've been for twenty years. I fought back tears through most of the meal and D was tearful, too. He hates to see me hurting. It was my final goodbye to David, and I already missed him. It's almost unbelievable that we'll never be that way again.

10/13/11: I worked on our letter to family and friends yesterday. I want it ready to mail next week. D wrote one for patients who have surgery or follow-up visits scheduled; the staff has been giving it out for weeks. He (DAMN! It's that pronoun thing again. I've got to remember it'll be <u>she</u> from now on) SHE wants to give patients the chance to cancel their appointments if they can't deal with the change. There's another letter going out today to medical staff. Soon they'll know that David isn't coming back; that it'll be Deborah presenting herself at grand rounds on the 26th. I can only imagine what will go through their heads for the next twelve days after they read the letter!

Yesterday was supposed to have been David's last day at the office—the final day of his male life before our twelve days off. He rushed home, excited to dress as Deborah for a cocktail party to kick-off the transition. After cocktails, we were taken to dinner by a bunch of the nurses and a couple of docs who've known about the impending change for a while. Everyone there, especially the nurses who all love David, is excited about the transition, but very few people seem to think about what this is like for me. I'm exhausted and don't feel like celebrating. Hell, I'm saying goodbye to my husband. I did my best to be upbeat (could be why they don't know that I'm struggling). I don't want to skip things like this, though. Folks need to know that I'm on-board with the change, despite what's going on with me internally.

D's at the office this morning, as David. He (she?) hated putting guys' clothes on again, but most folks don't know about Deborah yet, and there was paperwork to do before leaving for almost two weeks. I bet the office staff was surprised to see him. They've been so good since he told them about the transition; all seem accepting. They love him, too. We'll be taking them and their spouses to dinner next week, so they'll have a chance to see Deborah in person before she returns to work. When D gets home later, the transition begins in earnest.

Let's see: How am I doing today? Neutral, I think. Resigned. I'm in a "wait and see" mode. How could I be anything else? I just don't know what will happen, with us or the rest of the world. But I'm determined to support my sweetie through this and see where we go from here. We've definitely reached a point of no return. I'm so grateful that D is being attentive and caring—essential elements of this marriage. Otherwise, I couldn't go through with this.

10/15/11: Just a few minutes to myself, though I feel such a need to withdraw and have solitude. My entire life now revolves around the transition. Even my own projects—the book, choosing a book shepherd, the letter to family and friends—everything's about The Transsexual and The Change.

Had a session with Janet [my life coach] yesterday and, of course, she encouraged me to make time for myself. But it's harder to arrange, now that the cabin's closed for the season and I can't escape to our summer sanctuary. Today's "Daily Word" supports solitude: "Time apart is necessary for my well-being and my peace of mind." Amen!

My honey will be getting up soon and I've promised to assist her with dressing. (She's rarely been out so close to home, but the time has arrived.) We got her hair at The Hair Club for Women yesterday and it's amazing, though she needs to go back for adjustments today. But first, she has her nail appointment and ear piercing—everything she thought would be required to be a "real" woman! Then, after the hair is fixed, she'll pick me up and we'll go shopping for clothes. She has a job interview with a Maine hospital next week and will need more of a wardrobe for that. And soon she'll need things to wear every day as a professional woman.

Tomorrow I'll be with my MSIA group. It'll be time for me to refill my cup before we go to Maine for the interview, then head to the Cape for Fantasia Fair.

10/18/11: We're in a tiny town in Maine for Deb's interview. We got to this bed and breakfast last evening, after packing all morning and driving for three hours. When we checked-in, it was so odd. The proprietor asked whether we were okay sleeping in the same bed! That's a new one for us. The drive was relaxing and I felt more like celebrating, but now it's scary. We'll be joined at breakfast by the hospital's CEO & COO—both women! After breakfast they'll take Deb to the hospital to continue the interview. I'll pack-up, then a realtor is picking me up to show me the area.

It's only about 6:00 am, but I need to quit and help Debby get ready to shine. We can hardly believe this is happening! <u>Deborah</u> is having a job interview—<u>David is no more</u>.

10/19/11: Well, the interview went really well, even though I started to cry in the middle of it. I was telling them what our lives have been like and the tears just started falling. I can't even analyze this; it just happened. Amazingly, the CEO told Deb at breakfast, "You look beautiful!" I guess that's not enough, though. They've already let us know they hired someone else. I'm not sure that little town in upstate Maine is ready for a big, tall, transgender surgeon anyway. Deb is thrilled that she actually had the interview. Talk about her fantasy coming true!

It now looks like we'll stay in Gardner and see whether they can handle this. Nothing else is working-out, and we're running out of time. Maybe all those folks who've been encouraging David to stay after transitioning are right, but only time will tell.

We left for the Cape around 2:00 yesterday and spent the night in Kittery, Maine. Dinner was incredible, with both of us in tears of joy and wonder at what had been accomplished. I felt such love and pleasure at seeing my beloved living this dream, after all the years of fear and pain. I know some of my tears were for my loss, too.

Got to Provincetown in the late afternoon and checked into a really sweet condo. Thank God we'll have privacy. I'm so glad to have a space of our own so we can relax and recuperate a bit. We met our dear west coast friends for dinner and had the sweetest time—all the sweeter for their happiness for Deb and her transition this year.

10/22/11: We're already leaving Provincetown today, after just three days. Even so, we feel renewed, supported, and loved. We didn't attend many of the Fair events, having come for the friendship and to play with the people we love. They understand this whole thing better than anyone else. Ran into lots of folks we know on Commercial Street and they're all thrilled for Deb. Again, there's little (or no) interest in my process. No one even mentions it except our closest friends.

We skipped the Follies last night and brought some folks back to our condo for drinks and munchies instead. There's such diversity among the diverse! One wife has told her spouse of forty years that if he ever decides to transition, their marriage is over. She's been supportive of his cross-dressing for the twenty years she's known of it, but she says she must be married to a man. I appreciate that she knows where to draw the line; I almost envy the simplicity of her declaration! It's rigid, but could it somehow be better than my ambiguous, "I don't know what this will mean for us"?

The other couple last night attends lots of transgender events and we both think he'd like to transition, but they're pretty sure their families could never accept. There seems to be lots of fear in their situation. Most of their relatives don't have any idea that cross-dressing is part of this couple's life & marriage.

Our lone friend comes each year to cross-dress without his wife, though she supports him in attending the Fair. He says he has absolutely no desire to be a woman. For him, the dressing is just fun, relaxing, and a complete distraction from his successful, high-powered life (which he also loves). Deb cannot comprehend this blasé attitude! Our discussion was fascinating and the evening was rich and wonderful.

We need to head home shortly for tonight's dinner with Deb's office staff. It's hard to pack-up and leave this idyllic setting. I feel such comfort here among our kindred spirits!

10/23/11: I finished writing the announcement to family and friends yesterday and got about fifty into the mail. I'll send more by e-mail today. Composing the letter was challenging, since responses are completely unpredictable. It's scary, but it's a done deal now. Deb mailed her letters to patients and medical staff last week. I can just imagine the shock waves we've sent out! There's no turning back now. Soon, everyone will know. I'm resigned to whatever comes next, and I pray that this will be as smooth and grace-filled as possible.

∞

At the moment you are most in awe of all there is about life that you don't understand, you are closer to understanding it all than at any other time. –Jane Wagner

October, 2011

Our Dear Family and Friends,

This letter will come as a shock to many of you, as you have been unaware of the hidden life that David has lived since early childhood. When we met in 1987, David was cross-dressed and temporarily using the name "Deborah." Throughout our twenty-year marriage, David's cross-dressing has been an important and enjoyable part of our lives. We have an amazing community of transgender friends and couples.

Two years ago, it became apparent that cross-dressing was not the limit to David's transgenderism. We both realized that he is transsexual; that he truly feels like and wants to live as a woman. He began taking female hormones in fall 2009, and has since experienced the greatest happiness and satisfaction of his life.

This month Deborah will emerge full-time. The life of David is over; Deborah Rae Fabian, M.D., has taken his place. Though there will be no surgeries at this time, David has assumed the feminine gender role and, hereafter, will be legally known as Deborah (or Debby or Deb). She is currently revealing her new identity to the medical staff and patients.

All of our children have been told of the transition and their reactions vary. Each seems to be finding, or working toward, acceptance of their father/step-father in her new form. One of our greatest concerns is that some of you may drop out of our lives. We are hopeful that this won't happen, as you mean a great deal to us.

Please consider that this choice means the end to six decades of depression and longing in David. It will in no way alter the kindness, brilliance, warmth, and loving nature of this individual. In fact, these qualities are enhanced as Deborah's sadness falls away. We hope that you can be happy for her.

I am, for obvious reasons, having a transition of my own. While I've encouraged David to follow his soul's longing and I fully support this enormous change, I am experiencing a great sadness. The fact is, I am losing my husband. At the same time, I am comforted and supported in my grief by the same dear, incredible individual to whom I've been married for two decades. This is the paradox with which I am dealing. A Zen quote that assists me in accepting this and all of life's consistent permutations is: "If it's not paradoxical, it's not true."

Once you begin to absorb the meaning of our announcement, many obvious questions will arise. The answer to your first question is: *yes, we are staying together*. The love that we share, the commitment to our marriage and each other, transcend the form that we take. Nevertheless, in my desire to be completely honest with my mate, I have stated that I don't know what will happen with us in the future. We hope that we'll someday be two little old ladies growing old together, but only time will tell.

156

Of course, it's too soon to know how we, as a couple, will fit into society as our new form is presented to the world. Naturally, we are concerned about the reactions of the medical staff and Deborah's patients, as their rejection of Dr. Fabian's new gender would affect the status of our livelihood. It seems absurd to us that anyone would allow this transition to alter their appreciation of Deborah's surgical skills, but we are not so naïve as to think that there will be no negative responses.

The same concern applies to our family and friends. We love you and hope that your love for us will allow you to accept this situation.

With love and appreciation from us both,

Leslie

∞

10/24/11: The dinner with staff on Saturday was amazing! All of them, as well as their spouses, seem completely on-board with this transition. What a relief! They're highly concerned for me and my process, too—a nice change that warms my heart.

10/25/11: We had facials yesterday and Deb had her eyebrows waxed and tinted. It's bizarre, doing these girlie things with my spouse. I notice that calling her "my spouse" is what feels most comfortable. People ask me about this a lot. It just doesn't feel like my <u>husband</u> is now my wife. I'm still the wife in this relationship, and I feel sort of adamant about it.

Last night I came up with a good way to tell Deb that I need time to myself: "I'm in my tired room," I told her. It's better than bitching and it's a clear, kind statement that means *leave me alone!* Sometimes I just can't endure any more interaction, especially with all that's transpired these past ten days & all the people we've been with. I am so tired of it all!

The condo is quiet and all mine for awhile. Deb's getting her new driver's license and changing things at the bank and didn't need me to assist. I'm proud of her, doing things on her own. It's amazing, when I think of all the paranoia through the years. At least that's gone now. It's a relief to have her handling this without me, and she's relishing going out around town.

Thank God for my coaching with Janet. We've just had a session and I'd launched into a pressured description of all that we've done these past ten days. She reminded me to slow down and breathe, and suggested that my racing mind and speech are anxiety-driven. Of course they are! We also talked again about the necessity of my taking time for myself. It's been a frequent theme in our work; we both know I've <u>gotta</u> have it. My "Daily Word" helps again: "When challenges arise, I slow my pace. Grateful for the beauty that surrounds me, I continue on my way."

I can hardly believe that tomorrow's finally the day Dr. Debby reveals herself at the hospital. I've had waves of grief all morning—have been crying in bouts. It's the way I felt when Sandy and I split up and after my siblings died. It's good that I expected this and know it will pass, but I'm glad Deb's out for a while. She doesn't seem to understand that I need to cry. That even though it's happening a lot, it doesn't mean I have regrets or that anything needs to be done. It's grief, plain and simple. OMG, this hurts.

Later, on 10/25/11: I can't stay away from my journal. There's so much on my mind, and it relieves me to write it down. I suppose it helps me feel as if I have some sort of control. We've just planned everything for tomorrow morning: Deb's outfit, shoes, hair, makeup. Everything is laid-out. Grand rounds are at 8:00, so we'll be up early and out the door. I'm relieved to have reached this point at last, but I still wish I were miles away. No escaping now, Leslie. You've promoted and allowed all this!

Geez! This is bizarre! I can't get this song out of my head: Tammy Wynette's "Stand by Your Man"—in an all new version! I'll stand by all right, but I'm sure it's not what Tammy had in mind!

∞

CHAPTER TWENTY-ONE
GRAND ROUNDS

10/27/11: IT'S HAPPENED! Dr. Deborah Fabian is front and center now, and we're still living and breathing. She was amazing yesterday! She faced about a hundred people and told her story—and the reception was entirely positive!

As usual, when nervous or upset, she didn't sleep well the night before. I slept soundly, then popped awake at the crack of dawn, but I was still exhausted from all the emotions and our twelve days of "vacation." We were both really anxious, but we rallied and got her ready and on her way by 7:30. I felt like a stage mother! Fixed her hair, perfected her make-up, supervised preparations—all the while wondering whether I'll be expected to do this every day. What have I gotten myself into? I've got to get her trained to do this herself.

I arrived at the hospital by 8:00, and someone had saved a seat for me in the front row. I'm glad I got there at the last minute. I'd have been more of a nervous wreck if I'd had to sit there waiting for her to start. They'd moved walls to enlarge the room, but it was still packed. Standing room only! I guess after reading Deb's letter, nobody wanted to miss seeing her and hearing more. She said much of what she's presented in her church services, including the arrest, the suicidal thoughts, the whole story. Then everybody jumped up and clapped and cheered for her! It was absolutely amazing. The Heywood Hospital medical staff was supporting Deborah!

There wasn't much time for questions and discussion, but the comments were all positive. Several docs expressed gratitude for Debby's courage and honesty. They'd lacked information about transgenderism and have been frustrated, attempting to treat these patients. They were glad to know more, especially from a colleague.

Lots of folks lingered to congratulate Deb, to hug her or shake hands, so we only had time for a quick hug of our own—no private time to process what had just happened. I was so relieved and amazed, I was close to tears when a friend grabbed me and took me to breakfast. Everyone else rushed off to the business day ahead, including Debby. She told me later she'd been so focused on grand rounds, she hadn't even thought about preparing to see patients! But it went really well, again. No one had cancelled, despite her "warning" letter, and she had a full day of patients. Some of her patients didn't even mention the transition. Lots did comment, though, and they told Deb how much her letter had moved them. Some even told her how good she looked. This all seems absolutely miraculous to us both!

Last night was amazing. Deb came home, and we just kept rehashing and marveling at the wondrous experience we're having. Then, to relax, we watched the Robin Williams' movie, "What Dreams May Come," a mystical exploration of death, heaven, and soul mates. It touched us deeply, and we both wept as we watched it and recognized how much we love each other. We are so committed to this marriage of ours (and, of course, we're both totally exhausted by everything that's happened).

This has to be the ideal outcome, despite FEAR (those fanaticized experiences appearing real)! So far, it seems that all the negative fantasies are dissolving into the reality of loving acceptance and joy!! I am in awe.

It's almost impossible to overestimate the unimportance of most things.
—John Logue

∞

CHAPTER TWENTY-TWO
AFTERMATH

10/28/11: I'm headed to New Hampshire today to spend some time with Deb's parents, and it looks like I need to tell them about the transition. Now that D is living this way (with long hair, pierced ears, and red nails), there's no way to hide it from them. I can't believe we thought we'd get away with that! Announcing it on the phone wouldn't be fair (they can hardly hear, anyway), and Debby can't just waltz in their door and announce herself (but we've had fun imagining that)! So it falls to me to do this, and I'm okay with that.

I'm not sure I'll do it today. It's my decision and I need to see whether it feels right. Deb's just grateful I'm willing to do it. I know I'll have to explain it over and over to Mom, and I'm just so tired of talking about it. At least now I can share the book with her & that'll help explain things. She's been asking about my writing for months and I keep giving her other things I've written. Dad's been failing for some time and won't have any awareness of the conversation, so I'll just tell Mom. Then we'll figure out what to do about Dad.

10/29/11: Well, I did it! I told Mom about Debby. Her primary response: shock (of course); concern for me (not much for Deb); anger; dismay. She was most upset that she never had a clue about this and that no one had told her before. It didn't seem to make sense to her that very few others knew until recently. She thought she should have known. She had many, many questions, despite my telling her, "It's all in the book." She needed to talk, as I knew she would; it's understandable. But the revelations, discussions, explanations, and physical effort—on top of all the emotions I'm experiencing—are enough to put most people over the edge! I'm not sure how I'm managing this.

Deb's gone for a nail appointment, so the house is quiet and all mine now. I'm so grateful for the time and space to myself. This is my time for recovering.

10/30/1: It's not even Halloween yet, but it looks like January outside! Unbelievably, we had over a foot of snow yesterday. I'm trying to find a way to feel good about this—to enjoy its beauty (it is beautiful)—but it's not working. Despite all my gratitude and positivity, I am <u>not</u> happy with winter in October! It feels like too much to deal with, on top of everything else in my life right now.

I'm thinking about my brother this morning, deciding how I'll handle it if he can't accept the transition and my remaining with Deb. It's actually what I was afraid might happen, so I'm preparing to be okay with it. But it's so painful to think of losing my only remaining sibling. I think my heart's been broken enough that I'll be okay if it's over for us, but I just don't know when or whether to start the sad, undesirable process of accepting. I suppose it's like accepting snow in October—what choice do I have but to do it?

Deb called her mom last night for their first conversation since I'd told her the news, and it was pretty much what we'd expected. Mom wonders what she did wrong; she wonders why D has to do this; she doesn't want Dad to know, etc. She also said she needs a couple of weeks to get used to this before seeing Deborah. I wonder whether she understands how difficult David's life has been, whether she's happy for her child. She mentioned neither, just how shocked and confused she is.

I am committed to being as happy as I can be in my life, and now I have a truly happy mate, like never before! I'm reading *How to be Happy all the Time* by Paramhansa Yogananda and it's an absolute jewel, to wit: *It takes courage to renounce the known for the unknown. ...Life is change. ...Go forward from day to day with calm, inner faith.* Okay, that's my intention now. My path is just a tad rocky right now, but I'm keeping on!

I glance outside, see the morning sun shining on the tops of snow-covered evergreens, a pale blue sky as backdrop. Once again, I'm aware of the beauty and blessedness of my life, of the steady, unwavering presence of Spirit. I am grateful.

11/1/11: There have been blessings every day since the transition. We've had phone calls and messages, cards and e-mails; declarations of love and support from folks who've received our announcement letter. It's been a joy to hear a variety of voices on voice mail, cheering us on. Of course, some folks haven't responded at all, and we know that this is a message, too. But we were prepared for the worst. Most of what's occurred has been overwhelmingly positive. It feels miraculous!

Deb tells me daily about the good, kind things people say—patients and medical staff, even other hospital employees. Most speak of her courage, and a few have told her that her letter actually inspired them to heal unresolved differences with estranged family members! We are awed by the positive outcomes of what she's done.

11/2/11: I've not heard from my brother and am allowing this to be more and more okay, as I consider his departure from my life. I'm not interested in a relationship with anyone who cannot accept who I am or who my mate is. Meanwhile, everyone else has been accepting, except for a couple of young female patients who actually voiced their distaste for Deb's appearance, and whose parents just stood there and said <u>nothing</u>! We wonder whether they were expressing what their parents couldn't. It was just so rude and inappropriate.

11/4/11: Well, it's been over a week since the transition. The response has been overwhelmingly positive and Debby couldn't be happier, but now I find myself in an emotional tailspin. I think I was preparing to fight or flee for months; steeling myself, leading up to grand rounds. Then it happened and, unbelievably, everything was okay. I'm having trouble regaining my equilibrium, feeling balanced.

It's good that I've stopped seeing clients for awhile. I used to appreciate the way focusing on their issues removed me from some challenge in my own life, but I just don't have the energy right now to be with them the way I'd want to be. The cabin's closed for the next six months, so I can't run-off. I really need this time to myself, while Deb's at work, for the solitude and quiet.

These past two years of adjusting, preparing for Deb to come-out, telling people what was happening, explanations ad nauseum, seeing David gradually disappear and now be so easily accepted by others—it's left me reeling. I struggle with the absence of my husband, my man, my David. I must honor this grieving process I'm in. It's kind of like holing-up to recover and lick my wounds.

11/5/11: Another miracle: Last night Deb told me about a patient in his seventies who'd had surgery a couple years ago. He came in yesterday because he needs his other hip done, but said that he hadn't been sure he'd be okay with the transition. He said he'd actually sensed that David was really unhappy when they'd first met and then the letter had explained why. Turns out, he not only scheduled his next surgery, but he congratulated Deb and said he was really glad that she's finally happy!

There's also been a hospital employee who recently revealed concerns about a transgender child. She told Deb that, after years of fearing for her child, the letter had provided her with some real courage and hope! Now that she's witnessed what Deborah has done and has seen people accepting this transition, this mom has begun to believe that her child might actually have a happy life. Will wonders never cease? I hope not!

11/6/11: Deb's dad has been falling repeatedly and is now hospitalized. We need to go to New Hampshire and check on him and Mom, despite her edict that she won't be ready to see Deborah for awhile. We've decided we'll just start driving north and call her on the way. If she's not ready for her first encounter, Deb will go and do something else, and I'll take Mom to see Dad.

D called her brother yesterday, to tell him about Dad's situation, and it was really unpleasant. He seemed to speak for his whole family, including his daughters and their husbands, saying that everyone's upset and that no one wants to see Deborah. (He jumped right into this; they hadn't even discussed Dad's situation yet.) It amazes me to think that it's family members, those who I'd think would be most supportive and loving, who are having the greatest difficulty with this transition. I suppose this is perceived as a reflection on family; others can maintain a distance. Anyway, it sucks. But I'm developing thicker skin as a result and will go (with my beloved) in the direction of the folks who <u>do</u> love and support us!

11/8/11: Mom was amazing on Sunday. When we told her we were on our way, that we really needed to see Dad and talk to her about her next steps, she said she didn't know whether she could meet Deb yet. When we arrived, she said she guessed she was ready and had Deb step into the apartment. "Well, here you are," was her first comment. Then I asked, "What do you think of your new daughter, Mom?" and she told Deb, "I just can't believe it. You look pretty good, I guess." She wanted to get to the hospital right away, of course, to get to her husband. It was a good distraction, albeit a sad one.

Dad seemed about the same as he has for at least a year now—weak and dozing, then waking up and cracking jokes. He wanted to get up and go home. When we went in, Mom introduced Deb as a friend of mine, but Dad asked a couple of times, as we were sitting there, who she was. I'm sure she must have seemed familiar somehow. We're leaving it up to Mom to decide what to tell him. By the end of the day, when I asked Mom again what she thought of her daughter, she said she's decided to love the person on the inside! I'm really proud of her. At ninety-five, she's able to accept this profound change in one of her children—though I know she sees it as losing a son (as I've lost a husband). Here's the familial support we'd hoped for. Will the rest of the family can come-around? It's not looking good with the brothers.

I feel peaceful this morning, alone at home. I love the Zen Calendar reading, from LuYu: "The clouds above us join and separate, the breeze in the courtyard leaves and returns. Life is like that. So why not relax? Who can stop us from celebrating?" Yes, I can celebrate and nobody can stop me!

11/12/11: A couple of things keep coming up that we both find puzzling: Most folks seem surprised that we were so concerned, before the transition, about what the reaction would be. Someone said to me yesterday, "Why would you be so worried? Everybody knows about this now. It's 2011; we've all seen it on TV."

Well, it's great that everyone knows about it these days; but seeing something on TV and deciding you're okay with it is <u>way</u> different from accepting it in your friend or your neighbor or surgeon! Don't the TV shows talk about the fact that transsexuals are <u>killed</u>, simply for being different in this way? D's already lost a job over this, even before the transition. Could they really not imagine why we'd be scared?

The other thing that seems surprising is when people ask Deb, "How could you have waited so long to do this?" Every time she's given her talk, she's detailed the obstacles in her way, starting with growing up in the fifties and sixties—a completely different era. I know they're empathizing with the pain of Deb's sixty years in the closet, but did they miss the part about how David hated being transgender all those years? That he'd been arrested; had a wife who told him he was disgusting; that he's been hiding the cross-dressing for decades?

This is why I have this impulse to run-away so often. Dealing with repetitive questions like these just makes me nuts! (And it's why I don't think I'd be a very effective therapist right now, although maybe the distraction <u>would</u> be helpful.)

11/14/11: Fortunately, my grief seems to be easing as we proceed, as I've known it would. And Deb continues to be accepted, respected, and loved. Gardner has surprised us beyond our wildest dreams! I need to keep this in mind and remain calm with all the curiosity about it. These people are supporting my spouse (and me) and they want information. Haven't I always said that I want to educate? Remember that Leslie!

We went out to dinner last night and found that another waitress who knew us as Leslie and David is just fine with Deborah. This has been another amazing outcome—all the waitpeople we've come to know seem fascinated and curious, and no one's been rude or inappropriate in any way. The first time we went to our favorite seafood restaurant, it must not have been busy. Two of the waitresses pulled up chairs and sat right down with us to hear the story. It was hysterical!

One thing I've noticed is that women generally seem much more comfortable with this change than men. I've thought about this a lot. One of my theories is that women, those who like being women, anyway, can understand why a man would want to be one. They're fascinated. I'm guessing that most men, on the other hand, can't imagine wanting to become women. Why would a man want to give up his powerful position <u>as a man</u>? Of course, the only ones overtly expressing difficulty with the transition are our brothers. Deb's sister has been incredible from the start. Part of her process of accepting this has been a combination of sadness for her brother and pretty intense pain for herself. She'd always wanted a sister!

11/15/11: Today I feel unencumbered by the grief & huge concerns I/we had prior to the coming-out. Deb is happier than I <u>ever</u> saw David. She's even skipping her favorite morning ritual of reading the "Boston Globe" and doing the crossword in bed, getting up early enough to have her hair and make-up looking great. She seems to be enjoying the whole process, so far. The entire phenomenon is quite amazing in every respect. Patients and colleagues continue to be respectful and kind.

My primary on-going challenge is the info-sharing nearly everywhere I go. It's obvious that Gardner is a really a small town! Maybe people feel freer to ask me about the transition, rather than Deb. I had my teeth cleaned yesterday and had separate discussions about the transition with the hygienist, the dentist, <u>and</u> the front desk personnel. This continues to be exhausting, but I think it must be done. It's important to explain the situation, to let people know that I'm supporting my spouse. And there's so much misinformation out there, I do like educating people about this. (Keep breathing, Leslie!)

11/17/11: I need to watch my efforts to have Debby leaving for work every morning looking fabulous. She really wants to be doing most of it herself now, but I have trouble resisting the tweaking and redoing, especially when she asks for my appraisal before leaving. True, she doesn't have the background in making herself look feminine and professional, but I need to remember that not everyone has my standards. Besides, I've now decided (and Deb agrees) that my going south in January will be okay, that she'll be okay on her own when I leave. I need to back off! Yesterday one of the female docs at Heywood told Deb she's "putting the other female docs to shame" with her appearance. Incredible! She was thrilled, of course.

Today Yogananda advises: "Be neither elated nor depressed at anything outside yourself. Behold the passing spectacle of life with an even mind. For life's ups and downs are but waves on an ocean, constantly flowing." Will I ever have an even mind? It's something to keep aiming for, I reckon. It almost seems against my nature, but an even mind would be such a blessing.

11/23/11: I've hired a book shepherd, someone to guide me through this book-writing process. We've just had our first one-hour session and I'm thrilled! Chaz Bono, formerly Chastity, recently came-out and Judy [my book shepherd] had seen an interview with him and his partner. She'd noticed how little attention was given to Chaz's girlfriend, and she thinks partners of Ts are virtually ignored, while the Ts get most of the attention. This is right-on, of course—hence the book and hence my choice of Judy to shepherd me to publication.

11/25/11: Yesterday was Thanksgiving and it began oddly. I woke up feeling really irritated, and it took me a while to figure out what was going on. I was completely ready for the feast. The house was clean, the table set; it wasn't that. Then I realized it had been exactly a year since my brother was told about the transition (a year in advance), and he's still not communicated whether he'll embrace or reject us. Once I realized what was bugging me, I decided to write him a letter. Basically, I asked him what we could do to help with his decision; then I put it in a beautiful card I'd been saving that reads: "I would rather have a mind opened by wonder than one closed by belief." [Anahasta Joy Katkin] Doing this was a relief. It lifted the heaviness so I could enjoy the rest of the day. I'm tired of the ambiguity of not knowing where my own brother stands on this. At least Deb's brother was firm in his rejection; no ambiguity to deal with there. The day was wonderful. Since we had family plus an extra friend, there was plenty to do, and Deb was a most willing and kindly helper. There's no underestimating the benefits of the happiness that's resulted from her transition!

11/26/11: I'd sent the announcement letter to everyone on our Christmas card list, knowing that some folks were bound to have judgments, and we finally got our first overtly negative reaction. It's from some older cousins I've known all my life. Part of me is able to appreciate the time they spent on their response, but their letter is extremely opinionated, pontificating on D's selfishness and lack of self-discipline (as if David could simply have put this part of himself, herself, aside with just a little bit of self-control).

It begs a reply, but I'm wise enough to wait for awhile without reacting. I'm determined to use it as yet another opportunity for learning, upliftment, growth—and forgiveness. Mostly I'm sad and kind of embarrassed that there are those in my family who would be anything other than compassionate and accepting. Calling on Yogananda again: "Life's ups and downs are but waves.... Shun emotional involvement with them, while remaining calm." Okay, Leslie; this is just another little wave to shun. I am calm, I am calm, I am calm.

12/7/11: I spent the afternoon with Deborah's mom yesterday and she has a new concern about us. She asked me whether D now wants to be sexual with a man! I told her that Deb is in love with me, that changing her gender has not suddenly caused her to want to be with someone else. I don't quite get why people would assume this would happen, except that most folks don't realize that gender orientation and sexual identity are two different things. A transition like this doesn't turn off the love the individual has for an existing partner, at least not for us. This question has come up with others, so I guess we should expect it, and just keep explaining. When people ask Deb, she has a simple answer: "Leslie and I are madly in love. There's no one else I want to be with." Oh my God! There is still so much explaining to do!

12/12/11: I'm still giving Deb lots of assistance; like today, after she'd washed her hair. She had blown it dry all over the place, filling it with tangles. Then she needed help to comb it out and set it. I must watch my frustration with her. After all, she hasn't spent a lifetime going to beauty salons. Besides, David never cared much about the appearance of his hair. We're obviously still in a learning curve.

Mornings are so different now. Gone is the quiet-time in my meditation room, with David reading the paper, arising just minutes before his departure, jumping into his clothes, and racing out the door. There's still the racing, but now it's preceded by hair styling and clothing consultation, jewelry choices, stuff like that. It's a bit like helping a young woman prepare for a special event, every day! Well, soon D will be on her own, and I'll be heading south. Meanwhile, I can nurture an attitude of gentle, loving attention and patience for my darling.

I do notice fluctuations in my feelings about the permanence of Deborah. I often miss my Davey and feel so sad that he's never returning. But most of the time, it's just a fact of life to accept and live with. I think of my parents, adjusting to the after-effects of Mom's polio. They were just twenty-nine and thirty years old, lacking all the tools and self-awareness that D and I can access. It's almost unfathomable! Relatively speaking, this is a piece of cake.

12/14/11: I've been awake since 4:00 AM, having had a really creepy dream. I was driving along a high, elevated peninsula or causeway of rock, enjoying the exquisite scenery, remarking on its beauty to the two (unidentified) children in the car with me. Next thing I knew, we were plummeting head-first into the depths below, where a churning ocean was crashing onto rock pillars, which had huge vines or trees twisted around them. It woke me up and there was no chance of going back to sleep, so I finally got up to write about it.

This dream feels like a statement about life as I knew it, ending abruptly. I said goodbye to the children, knowing that this was our end. Is one of them innocence dying? Life as a "normal" woman in a "normal" marriage? The other child—normalcy? I am plunging to the depths, taking innocence & normalcy with me, and telling them—tenderly, it seems—goodbye. It felt incredibly symbolic and disturbing.

12/16/11: I'm in a new stage with the transition. Deb's okay; others are okay—but I feel as if a storm has passed and now I don't know what to do with myself. What did that dream kick-off? I realize I need some help with all this emotion.

Ok, I've just taken action: I e-mailed Janet to schedule a coaching session, and I'm also going to look for an Internal Family Systems [IFS] therapist. I've had a brief training in this method and just read the website, and I think it might be a perfect method to handle the many parts of myself that are screaming for attention. I need to address the angst and sadness and loss I'm feeling, recognizing there's a part of me that seems to need emergencies to handle. She's feeling cut-off and adrift, with no one or nothing requiring her attention. Then there's the part of me that's lost David. She's grieving and feeling helpless to have what she wants. There's also a part that's commanding me to get over this—to put it all aside. And I'm aware of yet another part that wants to be noticed. It's the part of me that bristles when someone tells Deborah how brave and courageous she is to make this transition, without acknowledging my role in it or what I've given-up. Good grief! WHO AM I TODAY??

12/17/11: I was feeling calmer, more centered this morning, probably because I took steps to handle all the feelings that have shown-up. Then Deb came in and I read yesterday's journal entry to her and got all stirred-up again, discussing it. Now she thinks she needs to fix it, but I've got to work through this with a neutral party. She actually asked me to let her know if I start feeling that I must have David come back. I wish she understood that this is about my need to deal with my own feelings, not about anything she needs to do differently.

We've been looking at houses for sale, now that it looks like we're staying in this area, but a part of me feels resistance to this. Perhaps I should stop thinking of buying a house until I feel more settled with my feelings and see what comes next for me. I'm fluctuating, sometimes angry, sometimes vulnerable; shaky, and uncertain. I'm all over the place right now! I feel like Alice in Wonderland, tumbling into a deep hole of unknown circumstances.

12/20/11: I've realized that I shouldn't drink when Deb and I are at home alone and I'm feeling so emotional. I had a glass of wine while fixing dinner last night and got really bitchy with her. Even a little alcohol gives me loose lips; then all the stuff simmering inside me comes flying out in nasty barbs.

She's being as caring and attentive as can be, but she still has some of the same old annoying habits as David. (Imagine!) She'd offered to help with dinner, but then she didn't do what I'd asked, despite several additional requests for the same damn thing. It was as though her offer of assistance was all that she felt was needed; then she went about her own business. Why does she bother offering if she has no intention of doing what I ask?! (This was typical of David, and becoming Debby hasn't changed that!)

I think my anger ties into that part of me that keeps demanding, "What about me? You're not paying attention to me! Don't I matter?" (But this usually applies to others, not my Deb.) My reactions were extreme, especially after one small drink— and very hurtful to her. I don't like it, but sometimes I can't seem to help it, so this is a major aspect of my seeking help. I need to address this part of me that seems to want to inflict on Deb.

12/21/11: It's the holidays, and I'm remembering what it was like as a kid four days before Christmas. The magical feelings usually return to me, but I just can't get there this year. There's too much stirred-up inside me to feel carefree. I'm okay—I'm just observing and accepting the disharmony inside me, but it sure is disappointing.

In addition to the grief of our brothers' reactions, we're now receiving some Christmas cards addressed only to me, as if I'm single. This really pisses me off! It seems especially cruel to exclude my spouse, as though we're not in this together. I must remember that many folks are still locked into their safe little worlds, incapable (?) of accepting that nature has included variations in the plan. I have such difficulty with the "highly religious" folks who don't seem to realize that it's all God's creation.

12/23/11: We decided to go to Washington for the holidays and visit one of the kids. We're in an apartment with our own space, and Deb's daughter has lots of events and meals planned for the three of us. D and I are lazing-around this morning after the long drive down yesterday.

I've come back into my essence this morning, after reading and contemplating Thomas Merton's beautiful words: "Sunrise is an event that calls forth solemn music in the very depths of [our] nature, as if one's whole being had to attune itself to the cosmos and praise God for the new day...." It's essential for me to have reminders like this—of the sacredness of life, the presence of Spirit, the hidden, yet accessible nature of all us crazy humans. I'm in gratitude for having returned to this part of myself; I feel precious in this moment. Methinks that the Christmas spirit has finally touched me!

12/28/11: Heading home today. We've had such a happy time! I notice that being out-of-town with Deb now feels more like our old norm than what's been happening at home. It's like the times we'd go away before the transition, and David would cross-dress for several days. That's made it easier for me to relax and let go of all the angst I've been feeling. The only thing missing is that David won't be returning to me when we get home.

I've looked back at my prayer for December and note its success, especially this part: "...to be at peace with what is; to be calm and relaxed throughout the holidays." It took awhile, but I made it. Thank you, Spirit!

12/29/11: I found a therapist who works with Ts and their families. Had my first appointment with her yesterday and I like her. It was really good to tell the story to someone who's there just for me, without needing to explain much about the transition. I talked about the times lately when I've snapped at Deb or needed to run off and be by myself; how angry and frustrated I get with all the explanations to others. After listening for awhile she said, "You probably know this, Leslie—your anger is healthy." I do know that, of course, but it's really nice to have someone "give me permission" to feel it, and the space in which to express it. I still face the paradox of being totally supportive of the transition, while also feeling angry about it and missing my husband. It feels impossible to justify that, when I'm the one who encouraged Deborah to emerge. But I do know that it needs expression, and I'm glad to have someone to assist with that.

What comes to mind is my willingness to move to Massachusetts with Sandy in 1979, then ending-up depressed from turning my anger inward. It didn't feel justified, so I wasn't able to acknowledge or express it. I'll never do that again! Now I've found a way to get the anger out without being a lunatic at home and bitching at Deb. It's just so unfair when I do that.

12/31/11: Last day of a momentous year: The year David "left" and Deborah came present full-time. There aren't many things that are bigger than that, I'd think, at least in terms of personal choices. As I write this, I realize immediately how this transition pales by comparison with cancer, war, terrorism, hunger, etc., etc., etc. How blessed we are to have the luxury of choosing this; a profession that is permitting it; a community that supports it. To have this freedom, to live in these changing times—such extraordinary blessings! "Daily Word" affirms a great start for 2012: "As I move forward, I bring with me the best of what was, and I create the best from what is. I am ready for a new beginning."

1/4/12: Hallelujah! I've just had a great coaching session with Janet, on top of seeing my therapist yesterday. Now I feel alive, enthusiastic, energetic, and grounded! Such a gift—the abundance of tools and guides to assist me in this crazy dance of life. I'm so grateful for the wherewithal to have asked for assistance all those years ago (nearly forty), when I was mired in postpartum depression. This has been my saving grace: Asking for help when I've needed it and receiving it!

Based on my talk with Janet, here are some things to watch for:

- taking care of Deborah so much of the time and expecting a pay-back of some kind
- anxiety related to my time spent making D look good (Is it scary to me somehow if she doesn't? What's that about?)
- learning to give enough to feel okay, without "over-giving" (creates anger, resentment, neediness)
- consider that I'm trying to create safety (that I didn't have as a kid?)

1/16/12: Gracie [our dog] & I are off to Florida today. The car's all packed and temps are in the single digits here. <u>It's time to go south</u>!

∽

CHAPTER TWENTY-THREE
AMBIGUITY, DETACHMENT, ACCEPTANCE

1/20/12: ARRIVED IN NAPLES YESTERDAY. It's gorgeous here—in the 60s and 70s. Heaven! I drove 1566 miles in four days, taking antibiotics for a cold. I'm pooped and not entirely well...but I'm warm. It's a relief to be away from all the hoopla at home. There's no one's hair and make-up to do each morning but my own!

1/28/12: Just a few more days in Naples, then I'm heading up to St. Augustine where I've rented an apartment. I've been working on the book a bit every day while in Naples and had a session with Judy [my book shepherd] yesterday. It really boosted my enthusiasm and I've agreed to her suggestion to write for three hours daily, once I'm settled in St. Augustine. That's my job now and I have no excuses whatsoever. I'm excited about this next phase of my 2012 get-away!

2/4/12: I felt really sad for awhile yesterday, missing David. I left Massachusetts nearly three weeks ago, and every time we talk on the phone, it's David's voice I hear. Mid-way through our conversations, I realize this is Debby I'm talking to. It's been really painful, remembering that my husband is gone. When I tell him about this awareness of mine, he still says he'll become David again if it means "keeping me." This continues to strike me as totally absurd, though I appreciate his willingness to sacrifice his new-found joy. Denying what has brought the most consistent and greatest happiness to D's life in sixty years, in order to maintain our relationship? Ridiculous. I don't want to live with a miserable man—and time, only, will tell me whether I can continue in this odd situation.

Part of what's going on is my desire for a man to make love to me. Despite my lack of libido, I do sometimes crave being wanted and desired by a man. Ah, another paradox: David's the one that I want, but he doesn't exist anymore!

2/6/12: I went to the St. Augustine U-U church yesterday; enjoyed the service and met a few folks. It's awkward to talk about my spouse now, after twenty years of referring to "him" or "David" or "my husband." When I meet someone and want to say that D is joining me here, I have to think fast about how to word it. I don't think of Deb as my wife. I just can't. I now say "my spouse." What's amusing is that people then automatically ask about "him," assuming I'm talking about a husband. I'm struggling with this. I used to have a husband.

That evening was the church's monthly event, feeding the homeless a home-cooked meal. I joined them and it felt good to be of service, something I've not done lately—unless, of course, supporting D's transition, grieving my loss, and writing a book about it all might just possibly be service!

I had a phone session with Judy this morning and spent quite a bit of time explaining the difference between sexual orientation and gender identity. As with most folks, it's confusing to her. She's not heard Deb's talk, explaining that being transgender is about who she is, not who she's sleeps with.

2/10/12: Deb is coming down next week. I continue to miss <u>David</u>, and I keep forgetting he no longer exists. I just don't think of it as missing Deborah. It'll be good to be together, though I don't seem to be feeling as alone this year as I did last year. This must be about my desire for David to return to me—a useless yearning. Interesting that I use that term. David wrote and spoke of his yearning to be a woman. I am now yearning to be with my husband, who is no more.

Some part of me feels that we won't go on indefinitely, as a couple. It's odd and a little scary to write this. I'm aware that one huge role I played in David's life was to assist him in gaining self-acceptance; to be able to allow Deborah to emerge full-time; to allow him this freedom and provide support for this transition.

What if I begin to know, in my gut, that our time together—our marriage—is over? D has said so many times, "I don't want to lose you," but I don't know that I'll be able to continue this. Perhaps this is because we've been apart for nearly a month now? We'll see how it goes when we are together, in less than a week.

2/16/12: Deb is with me now and she's taking a nap. She arrived around noon and, so far, the visit has been a mixed-bag. As I drove to the Jacksonville airport, I prepared myself to meet her—but what I really wanted was to be meeting David. There's a dream-like quality to this, as if I can awaken from all that's transpired in the past four months and have my husband back. That's magical thinking, I know.

On the way back, we stopped at the outlet shops to get her some warm-weather clothes and have lunch, which was fun. But I realized it was like being with a woman friend. When we got to the apartment, she pulled me down on the bed, but I couldn't get over that feeling that I was with another woman, not my lover. It just didn't feel right. I wasn't aroused at all and had to tell her. She was devastated. She cried a lot—far more than David ever did. I think she felt betrayed, somehow. She'd gone to a transgender support group last night and told them that everything is wonderful with us. I don't disagree, exactly. I just see that the nature of our relationship has changed. How could it not change?

When I told her how I felt about being sexual with her today, she asked me whether she should go back home! This reminds me of the times I'd ask for what I wanted sexually, and David would automatically interpret this to mean that I wanted the cross-dressing to stop. Of course I don't want her to leave! Why must she go into over-kill?

I'm feeling calm and neutral about this, though I'm sad that D feels so hurt and frustrated. She finally has her dream-come-true, but it may be that I will not continue to be her lover, as she wants. I certainly have no desire to be with anyone else, but I think we are redefining this marriage—or I am, anyway. Again, how could I not be?

2/17/12: Things got better last evening. We had a wonderful dinner at a little Italian restaurant, then drove to the historic district of St. Augustine, so D could see some of this beautiful, old town. I truly no longer feel as though D is my lover. In fact, we'd not made love for weeks before I left for Florida. This seems okay to me now (though I never dreamed I'd be neutral about sex) and I'm observing the shift that's taken place: We are the dearest of friends, with a closeness unparalleled—but, at the moment, I just don't feel married anymore. I'm not sure yet whether to share this (a huge withhold) or wait awhile, to see what transpires. I'm so glad we have time for playing and relaxing together.

What's interesting is D's interpretation of how well we've been doing since October. As far as I'm concerned, we're in a "holding pattern" in our relationship—it's a wait-&-see period for me. I love this person and am supporting all this change, so of course it seems we're doing well. But I still can't possibly know what lies ahead. To me, every day feels new for us, as a couple. To her, I guess "doing well" means everything is fine and dandy; that I've completely accepted the transition and our marriage as two women. This is far from true for me.

2/18/12: Yesterday was a great day that ended poorly. We'd driven to Orlando and checked into a hotel, then I'd consumed three glasses of wine throughout the evening. This was way too much alcohol for me, especially with so much simmering below my surface. It was certainly not conducive to my being rational and loving,

First, I got annoyed at Deb's making no response when I spoke to her. Then I felt hurt about Valentine's Day, which she hadn't acknowledged in any way. No gift or even a card, though she knew I had something for her. These are both old challenges of ours: Her lack of response when I've spoken to her, giving no indication she's even heard me, and her forgetting that holidays are important to me. I like to have them commemorated in some way. I know that feelings about the transition (and the wine I'd consumed) underlie all of this, but I just couldn't seem to stop my irritation.

We'd argued, then gone to bed. Ultimately, I felt so hurt that I got in the other bed, too upset to sleep with her. Of course, we both had a crappy night. Awake at 5:30 this morning, I listened to a forgiveness meditation on my iPod. This, plus being rested, enabled me to crawl back into bed with D, snuggle-up, and explain why I'd been so hurt. She had gone to the extreme (again) of thinking that she should pack-up and go home early. It's our old Catch-22 scenario: I'm hurt and angry, and she withdraws, increasing my hurt and anger, causing her to withdraw further. I guess transitioning doesn't automatically take away her "Martian" traits. She's still a lot like a guy.

We're having a rocky time, after our month apart and my having left home so soon after the transition. These circumstances are (obviously) not promoting extreme intimacy and closeness. Part of this, I'm sure, is my pleasure in solitude and the escape from the craziness at home. It feels a bit as though Deb has invaded my space, and that's not a good feeling at all. I do aim to get above this, so I can change my attitude and resume a rational perspective.

2/20/12: Things are improving for D and me as time passes, thank God. It's occurred to me that Deborah's constant presence and the absence of David is still very new, relative to twenty+ years of mostly David and just a little Deborah. And since I'd not been with my spouse for about a month, it's reasonable that there'd be some rough spots. The trick is to remember and allow for this in the future, without going to the extreme of fantasizing the end of our relationship.

Saturday and Sunday were happy days; now we both feel as though we're having a real vacation. We spent the day at Epcot on Saturday and I was proud of Deb for being so absolutely accepting of herself as we walked around the park. She's going everywhere now without hesitation or much insecurity. We're both relaxing and enjoying each other, but it really is like being with my dearest woman friend. The maleness that I loved in David—have loved in other men in the past—is gone. There's nothing sexual about our relationship right now, and the attraction is gone, too.

We went to the UU church yesterday and the topic was racism and discrimination in the United States. This church invites parishioners to comment immediately after the homily; so Deb stood up and told them, briefly, about the transition and of how strange it feels when she knows that people are looking at her and wondering about her. It was helpful that she did this. We were both wondering how to handle the "trans thing" with these folks. It led to lots of good discussion at the coffee hour and handled my discomfort with what to tell people there. I'm thankful that I'm okay with Deb speaking-up. Otherwise I'd have been mortified when she hopped-up and shared!

2/22/12: Debby left yesterday and her visit was (eventually) a delight, after the bumps of the first couple of days. I've realized that we simply cannot realistically expect what's occurred in our lives to mean that all will continue as before. I knew this, yet still felt unprepared. It's not surprising that there were some rough moments, though D seems to continue the black and white thinking that was David's style: "I'm happy, I'm accepted, Leslie's supporting me and my transition...therefore, everything is just fine."

2/23/12: Deb and I have just spoken and, despite having just been with her, I went right back to feeling as though I was talking to my beloved David. I cannot believe how readily I slip back into that. It's comforting to hear my husband's voice, though I'm completely aware that I no longer have a husband!

Deb was on-call last night and treated a man who'd had a car accident. The man's son had come to the emergency room, and they both began referring to Deb as "he," even though she told them a couple of times that it's "she" (and she looks female). Obviously, I'm not the only one who has trouble with her deep voice. I think that regardless of her appearance, when people hear the male timbre of her voice, they think (feel?) they're talking to a man. After she'd told me this and I'd had the sensation of hearing "him" on the phone, I told her I think she's got to change her voice if she wants to pass as female. Otherwise she may be correcting people forever. She's tried to sound more female, but says it takes a lot of effort; so I don't know that she'll bother.

3/1/12: My time was up in the St. Augustine apartment, so I left for Naples yesterday. It was a long drive, broken-up by lunch with old friends along the way. As usual, the discussion was dominated by talk of D's transition. Fortunately, my fatigue and initial discombobulation have passed in this month of solitude. It's easier to talk about it and answer all the questions that naturally arise, and it also seems to help with my own acceptance and integration.

3/3/12: I'm with my kids in Naples again. We had dinner with some of their good friends last night and I'd forgotten my daughter hadn't said anything to them about the transition. (She'd been concerned about their acceptance.) One of them asked me where David was and I said, "Well, first of all, David's Deborah now." Of course, this friend had no idea what I was talking about and it was an incredibly uncomfortable and confusing moment. (The expression on her face was priceless!) Then I'd explained everything and answered a multitude of questions, once again realizing that this topic had become the focus of the gathering. I'm definitely less frazzled now when talking about this, but it's certainly wearying, explaining over and over again. Still, it's an opportunity to educate and possibly open some minds.

3/5/12: I read several chapters of the book to my daughter and her husband on Saturday and couldn't help crying as I read. It all comes so present when I read aloud, there's no holding the feelings in. It's part of my healing and acceptance process, I suppose. I can't help wondering whether all these feelings will ever subside, though I've been through enough in my life to realize that nothing stays the same for long.

3/6/12: Spent last night in Tampa and had lunch with two high school friends. I'd sent the transition announcement to one of them, but the other hadn't known. So, once again I found myself explaining it all. They were both wonderful. Could it be that we've all lived long enough, been through enough, to understand that life is full of change and unexpected circumstances? Whatever it is, it sure feels good to tell old friends who accept and at least try to understand!

3/8/12: It's just occurred to me that getting away from the transition, even from Deborah, has been like a tonic for my soul. I do love my solitude. Too much, perhaps? Then again, who's to decide this but me? Maybe somewhat separate lives are what we need, though I'm sure Deb would disagree. I remember David's reaction to my wanting my own apartment years ago, when my kids were grown and he was still, basically, enmeshed in his children's lives. He was angry that I wanted that and would have none of it. Deb would be devastated to think that I'd want this now.

3/23/12: I'm on my way home now. Spent the night in Alexandria, Virginia, and had dinner with Deb's Washington daughter last night. She continues to be amazingly accepting of her dad's new status; calls Deb "Dad-X"—and D seems to like that. It's odd, what the kids now call their dad. When we're out with them around other people and they call her "Dad," I'm uncomfortable; but Deb doesn't seem to mind. I guess the relief of knowing they're okay with the transition removes all concern about that. To me, it's a question of respect for her; but I need to keep in mind the incredible fact that they've accepted their father's transition.

I've been rereading the Don Miguel Ruiz book, *The Four Agreements*, and read a quote this morning that touches me: "True freedom has to do with the human spirit—it is the freedom to be who we really are." Isn't this precisely what Debby and I are both doing in this crazy life of ours?

3/24/12: I got home last night and this morning I'm back to coaching D on her appearance. Seems like I'm right back where I was in January! Deb is on-call and needs to go to the hospital, and she's having a photo taken for the hospital web-site. She <u>says</u> she wants to look good for the picture, but I've got to convince her that she needs to make more effort—as most of us do, if we want to look good. (Especially at 62!) I don't want to nag. If she'd said she didn't care, I'd start working on not caring either. But if she wants to improve and wants to pass, she's got to make more effort! There was no sex last night. I just can't do it and D's not pushing it. Snuggling will have to suffice until something changes—if it does.

3/27/12: Life has been crazy since my return to Massachusetts. Deb's dad died on Sunday, after months on the decline, so now I'm in New Hampshire for a couple of days, to support Mom and plan a service. On Sunday, before we'd heard about Dad, Deb did a church service in another town, at the request of the hospital CEO. She's told her story once again.

3/29/12: I'm back from NH, and Deb wants me to set her hair. I'm already tired (again) of all the effort I make to improve her looks. I recall an old therapist once asking me why I care so much about David's appearance. He wondered whether it was for D's benefit or mine. That was good food for thought. Was it about wanting the best for my mate? Or about how I'd look <u>with</u> him...now <u>her</u>? Why do I care so much about this?

We're in a re-entry process. My solitude has evaporated, and life as a partner/daughter-in-law/responsible person has resumed. I want to get back to my writing, but I'm planning to create a collage of photos for Dad's service, as well as deciding what to say for the service (which I'm leading). Talk about a change of focus!

4/4/12: Saturday was a wonderful day of remembering Dad. Of course, this was the first time some of the family had seen Deborah, so there were some interesting moments. Her brother & sister-in-law came from Europe, and we'd invited D's ex-wife, too. Deb's brother was pleasant, but the women barely spoke to her—and she was fine with this. She's so happy and self-accepting now, she won't let anyone's response (or lack thereof) bother her. Deb's boys were there, too, and her sister and nephews. All of them seemed fine with Deb. It felt like we were marking a double milestone: Dad's death, Deborah's birth.

4/6/12: I'm having trouble balancing my time for journaling and spiritual centering with the needed effort to get this book written. It's time to accept that the book must take precedence in my life, though I won't neglect my connection to Spirit, either. I need time to acknowledge and revel in that; for meditation and a focus on gratitude, too. All of this enables me to accept our new life; and perhaps one day soon, I'll <u>flow</u> with it.

4/9/12: Deb's received notice that the complaints to the Connecticut Human Rights Commission about loss of the job there have been retained for further investigation. (It was possible that the complaint would have been dismissed.) A mediation meeting is planned for May 7th. This is heartening news.

4/20/12: As time goes by with Deborah, it seems more and more as if our relationship will continue, though it's Platonic now. Allowing this to be what it is, without a need to leave it or change it, may be the way to go. I feel that I've run the course with mourning my lost husband and am settling into this "something different," though it defies definition.

Hmm...I got up for another cup of tea and, when I got back and read what I'd written earlier, I realized that it's inaccurate to call our relationship "Platonic." Though we've not been sexual in months, it seems that our relationship is more than that (unless I'm unaware of the real meaning of the term). I think that we're lovers in a greater sense than just sexual. I wonder whether there's a name for this kind of thing—or are we inventing it?

4/22/12: We went to an open mic[rophone] at the church last night and both participated. I read a couple chapters of the book aloud and it was well-received. As usual, when reading it to others, I couldn't help crying—but I just plowed on through it. Deb cracked everybody up with her rendition of "Broken Bones, the Musical," something she made up for her improvisational acting class. It's hysterical! Good comic relief after my reading.

4/27/12: I'm thinking of my brother again, of the appearance that he's slipped from my life. He's not actually told me he's gone, but it seems apparent, based on his e-mails of a year ago and a lack of contact for some time. It seems that his love doesn't extend to accepting differences, but I don't know what to do about it if he doesn't give me an opportunity to address it with him. I would love it if he'd just call and ask me how I'm doing, but the thought that I'm struggling doesn't seem to have occurred to him!

I've picked-up Thomas Merton and found some insight into the question of trying to understand everything—or anything, really: "…I felt as if I had found a new center: something I could not grasp or understand…so I grasp at nothing and understand nothing and am immensely happy." All righty, then; there's a key to happiness! How wonderful to reach the point of simply not needing to know, or interpret, or name whatever is. This is the neutrality I seek, that tolerance for ambiguity and comfort with simply not knowing!

4/30/12: Yesterday I read all the documents related to Deb's case against the Connecticut hospital and the recruiting company in North Carolina. Mediation takes place in a week. The entire situation seems ludicrous, especially now that Deb's been practicing successfully in Gardner for six months without incident. How different our lives would be now, had that hospital not been so narrow-minded, with the recruiters colluding with them. We'd have two-thirds of every month to be anywhere, doing anything. Ah, well, they may end up paying for their discrimination, but it certainly doesn't feel good to be facing this. It's not something either of us has ever experienced before. My "Daily Word" encourages me: "I release any struggle and trust that my life is unfolding in divine order. I remain at peace with what is and listen for divine direction."

5/3/12: Deb joined me for a workshop last night called "Detachment and Freedom." For the first time, I heard my sweetie say that her transitioning is courageous! For some reason, she's not seen it in this way and has resisted the concept whenever others have suggested it and admired her for it. Funny, I can readily acknowledge my own courage, especially in supporting this crazy spouse of mine and staying married! There's certainly no question about her courage; maybe she's finally ready to acknowledge it.

5/7/12: We're in Hartford, headed to the Connecticut Human Rights Commission for mediation with the CT hospital and the recruiters. Our lawyer is optimistic, though he's warned us that nothing may happen today. If nothing does, we will be suing the hospital and recruiters. We've decided to proceed with this because we can, unlike so many others who've lost jobs and lacked the means to pursue it. We're ready to make a splash, for our own benefit and that of all transgender folks who've been mistreated in this way.

5/8/12: We were finished in CT just after noon yesterday, with unremarkable results. It was a fascinating process, with lawyers for the hospital and the recruiter, plus an insurance agent, in one room; us, with our lawyer (and his wife, also a lawyer), in another. A mediator ran back and forth between the rooms. She presented our desired amounts of compensation to the other parties, and the lawyer for the hospital refused outright. (The mediator had said he'd probably make a counter-offer, but he simply said, "No way," with no return amount for us to consider.) It's still unbelievable to us that they don't seem to think discrimination has taken place, so we will be taking them to court.

The recruiters are still considering our "demand": A settlement amount, plus a hospitalist job that meets our approval, or a larger sum and no job. We are still drawn to the idea of Deb working as a hospitalist, which would mean much shorter hours than she now works. Of course, if they don't find one for her—with all of her qualifications and experience—won't that prove that discrimination is taking place?

5/13/12: We cleaned out the garage yesterday and I'm on a roll. Now I'm ready to dispose of David's clothes, but Deb doesn't seem interested in participating. I would think she'd want to get rid of them herself, but no such luck. If it's going to get done, I'll be doing it. This task repels me in the same way that a widow might view disposing of her dead husband's belongings. Holding onto them doesn't bring the man back, but there's something comforting about having them near-by. I suppose this will be important for me—a huge step in letting go of the husband I once had, which is most likely why I've been avoiding it, and why a widow would put it off.

5/15/12: Man! I've just realized that two days of writing, reading, and rewriting the chapter about my life has me all stirred-up. Of course, getting rid of David's clothes compounded my angst. I do find that reviewing my life helps me keep D's transition in perspective. Really, the transition almost seems like a minor blip in my life, relative to some of the stuff I've lived through! Still, I'm agitated and I see a need for large doses of self-compassion and gentleness with myself.

5/18/12: We went out for a wonderful dinner last night for my birthday, and I found that I'm grateful for all the years of going out with a cross-dressed husband. In some ways, it feels the same, except I don't get David back when we get home (even if it is my birthday). It's become amusing to watch how new waitpeople deal with us. I think they may assume that I'm accompanying a transgender friend or that we're two women friends, if Deb passes. Then one of us will say something about our kids or how long we've been married; something that confuses them. I like the mystery about us and wondering what people think! Most folks are so locked into their assumptions, I like shaking them up a bit. This relationship continues to get easier all the time. My life with Deb seems to be working and I am usually a happy camper these days. Basically, I just can't imagine our not being together!

5/23/12: It's our anniversary weekend and we're going to Rowe [Conference Center in Rowe, Massachusetts] for the annual Memorial Day couples' workshop, offered by Joyce and Barry

Vissell. We want to make sure we're not missing anything that needs to be addressed. This will be our fourth or fifth time working with them. We've shared about the cross-dressing in the past, but this will be the first time since Debby has existed full-time.

5/26/12: Today is our twenty-first anniversary. It's fun to be here to do this work when we're in such a good place in our relationship, in spite of the transition. The best things I heard from Joyce and Barry today: When we're in disagreement, we must each reach a point of asking ourselves, "What did I do to step out of my loving?" We each need to take responsibility for our roles in conflicts. When we're hurt, they suggest saying to our partners, "I trust that you didn't intend to hurt me, but that was hurtful." I love the Vissells' way of dealing with problems that arise—and sometimes this happens right in front of us. I love that they're so real.

5/27/12: I'm so pleased and feel so blessed that Debby and I have reached this point in our loving. We know each other; we trust each other; we're comfortable with each other. We also know how to work-through whatever comes up for us, and we're willing to do it.

Last evening, Joyce and Barry honored us and our anniversary. They had us stand in front of the group, facing each other, and make new vows. It became a very tender recitation of our original wedding vows (the ones we could remember, anyway) and it's what we already do in our marriage most of the time. It was very sweet and affirming to make these vows in front of the other couples, and of course we plan to continue doing these things. What I love about this weekend is taking the time to concentrate on the intentions for our relationship. It's conscious loving, a conscious marriage, a la the Vissells and Harville Hendrix.

5/28/12: Today is the final day of Joyce and Barry's workshop. It's been an extraordinary weekend, as always, and what needed to come up finally surfaced yesterday: Our sexual issues. The two of us had a really good talk about it first. Then I shared with the group, with Deb's permission. What somehow developed was a focus on Deborah's shame about her very existence, and her lifelong desire to make the Trans issue go away. The Vissells brought her up front, then asked all the women to come and sit around her, for support, while they worked with her on her life-long shame. This has probably been the greatest obstacle in D's life—and, yes; her sexual expression has been all tied-up in shameful feelings. The work seemed to free her like nothing else has. Meanwhile, feeling totally vulnerable in revealing our sexual issues, I felt abandoned when Deb left me to go up front. Another couple we'd met years before stayed with me and held me, thank God. They'd apparently sensed my extremely fragile state. So, Debby made great strides—though our sexual issues were not adequately addressed. I know we'll eventually work through them, but it was disappointing to have the focus change so dramatically. Once again, this seemed like one of those times that my needs, as the wife of the T, were minimized.

One of the last things the Vissells had each of us do yesterday was to think of something special we'd like to say to our mates. Then each couple stood in front of the group and told their partners, with the other couples witnessing. Deb promised always to see and honor the playful or hurt child I am expressing. And I said something I hadn't ever before. I told her that I am now committed to her, to us, for life! This is huge!! When we married, we'd each said, "As long as we both are able." And since she began the female hormones, it's been, "I don't know what will happen with us." I think I was as surprised as Deb that I did this...and I meant it with all my heart.

5/30/12: I can hardly believe the anniversary card we got from Deb's mom—and this is the woman we were afraid to tell about the transition! She's handled it better than we ever imagined possible. It's a generic card, reading: "Remember you're cared for in a very special way." She'd added: "...by your mom and the others who can't be here now, and still others who aren't quite smart enough to have realized what a marvelous marriage you have carved out for each other. What a wonderful thing to do for us all. Happy anniversary!" We're amazed by her acceptance—and she's gone beyond just accepting, understanding how much we love each other. Incredible!

5/31/12: I need to prepare for a presentation Deb and I are giving this weekend. We're joining another woman who's written a book for transsexuals about transitioning. The three of us are presenting to a group of Internal Family System therapists, so they'll know more about treating transgender individuals and couples.

6/5/12: Saturday was a wonderful day, with seventeen IFS therapists, plus Anne Boedecker, author of *The Transgender Guidebook: Keys to a Successful Transition*. Anne described her work with the transgendered, Deb shared her life-story, and I talked about our relationship and surviving the transition. Our presentations were well-received, generating lots of interesting questions and comments. Here is some of what I said:

I begin with a quote from the Baal Shem Tov:

> From every human being there rises a light that reaches straight to heaven. And when two souls that are destined to be together find each other, their streams of light flow together, and a single brighter light goes forth from their united being.

Deborah and I believe that this is true of us, and my book has emerged from this greater light as our love story.

Needless-to-say, there is no one transgender tale, no one couple's story that will universally apply to all of us in this situation. Just as every client and couple whom you treat is different from the next, Deborah and I have a story that is unique to us. We are willing to talk about it, in the hope that our narrative may assist you in working with others who are similar to us. Because we have worked hard at this marriage, with its unusual features, for more than two decades, we may help to increase your knowledge and enhance your efforts in assisting transgender clients and their partners.

The transgendered face an enormous challenge in determining when and how to tell potential partners of their proclivity. Imagine, for a moment, wondering whether to reveal this secret upon first meeting; or on the third date; or waiting until attraction is giving-way to real love. When might you risk losing the one to whom you are attracted? In the beginning? Or later, when there's more to lose? Many of the transgendered are actually married for years, or decades, before revealing this part of themselves. When spouses are eventually told, there can be overwhelming feelings of betrayal, as well as doubts about honesty regarding other things that may have been withheld. Some never tell at all.

Since meeting David—I will refer to my spouse as "David" when speaking of times prior to the October 2011, transition—since our meeting in 1987, I've sometimes explained to others that our first encounter was the ideal, for a woman who will knowingly be married to a cross-dresser. This is because, when I met David at a gathering at the home of my friend Niela Miller, he was cross-dressed as Deborah. I was immediately aware of his greatest, most shameful secret. At the time, he was unaware that he'd eventually transition to female.

There was never a need for David to figure out how to tell me that he loved wearing women's clothing. Furthermore, because he was speaking at our gathering about being transgender and had revealed much of his life story, I was well-informed by the end of the evening. I was also smitten by this captivating individual. In my book, you'll find the long, intricate story of what followed our first meeting.

Eventually, after eighteen years of marriage, I realized that there was a way for my spouse to be truly happy: To live as Deborah full-time. I simply had to encourage it, despite losing the configuration that had made me happiest.

Yogananda had this to say about marital happiness:

> People who actually do find happiness in marriage don't find their happiness from one another. Always, it comes from inside themselves. How sad it is to see the suffering

people go through, just because they base their expectations of happiness in other people!

I am able to support this transition for my mate's happiness because I am not dependent on her for my own joy. I am aware that what she has done is not against me; it's for her. I'm reasonably certain that this is not something I'd have encouraged or accepted in my mate earlier in life, so I have compassion for those who are dealing with such an enormous change at younger ages, especially those with young children.

From talking with other transgender couples at Fantasia Fair and through my reading, particularly Helen Boyd's My Husband, Betty *and* She's Not the Man I Married, *I am aware that many wives of cross-dressers have one great fear: That eventually their husbands will realize that they are transsexual; that they will want to become women. This is what has happened with us. This is where we are now, and it looks and feels like it's working!*

∽◯♡

6/9/12: I'm feeling really uncomfortable this morning, despite being at the cabin, on the dock, with a stunning summer day before me. I had a disturbing dream, just before waking. My son was a toddler again, and we were laughing as we ran up a hill together. Suddenly, he was in a big hole, like a sinkhole. He was lying, face-up, in murky liquid. He wasn't getting up, though I was shouting, "Come on—get up! Come on!" I jumped into the hole and was trying desperately to pull him out, then I woke up. It was as if this hole had suddenly grabbed my child and was consuming him. I couldn't stop it. I was losing him. I can't understand how it happened—I was right there all the time. The feelings I notice: Futility, shock, frustration, surprise, fear, helplessness. Of course, this has something to do with the transition. Everything seems to. Maybe it's that I can't get my husband back, no matter what I say or do. And I was right there all the time, as he went away.

One thing is certain: I still miss David. Our life is so
different from before. I used to spend a week, at most, with
Deborah; then my husband returned. Now Deborah appears at the
end of each day and the "dream" continues. The energy has
changed. That chemistry that underlies attraction and desire is
gone. I miss what I felt for all those years. There are waves of
missing him—the grief process, of course—though I've thought,
at times, that I was through with it. Now I'm at the cabin for my
first summer without David. Something more to adjust to.

6/17/12: I've been at the cabin all week, writing and loving my
solitude. Debby joined me last night, and this morning, I focused
on just being with her. These times together on the island have
always been so valuable and sweet—a necessity to maintain our
loving connection.

I'd been reading through journals leading up to the beginning
of the transition and decided to share some of that old stuff with
Deb. It was painful, at times, eliciting more apologies from my
sweetie. (Whenever I'm having a hard time, she apologizes over and
over.) It was especially interesting to recall how things were in
2008, leading up to the beginning of the hormones. David was angry
and pretty obnoxious much of the time. It was hard to be with him.
It's no wonder that suggesting hormones seemed the reasonable
solution. She'd been denying her true self for way too long.

We had a very tender talk, then ate breakfast and played
cards outside on the deck, with the sparkling expanse of lake
below us. It's Father's Day and the kids have been calling. One
called yesterday and said she'd declared it "Transgender Parent's
Day." She said that Hallmark had been notified! How cute is that?
What a blessing it is. All the kids are hanging-in there with us and,
obviously, maintaining a sense of humor. Thank you, Spirit!

6/26/12: We've just been told that the condo we've been renting
since last summer is being sold. For some reason, we're both
feeling calm about this. Maybe we're just not surprised by
anything anymore! We need to be out by the end of July,
meaning more transition and ambiguity for our lives. We could
buy the condo, but we keep hoping that a hospitalist job in

another area will be offered, so we won't. Are we being naïve? We've heard nothing from the recruiters about a hospitalist job, and the lawsuit with the Connecticut hospital is still up in the air. Once the matter is released by the CT Human Rights Commission, we can proceed with it. One day at a time, Leslie. Keep breathing!

6/27/12: It's a gloomy day. Not usually bothersome to me, but I feel really annoyed by it today. Is everything going to bug me this year? Maybe I need to look deeper for reasons for this agitation. It's the underlying grief and adjustment process, of course (how long will this go on?)—and more than a few upcoming changes. I must remember to be gentle with myself; my life was turned on its head not long ago. This is exactly what you'd be telling a client, Miss Leslie!

6/29/12: The book is progressing and I'm happy with it, though I'm still writing about the time prior to Deb's coming-out. It already seems so long ago. It's been said that writers live twice— once going through things and again, while writing them, and now I understand. This must be why I'm struggling these days.

6/30/12: We now have a month to pack-up and move again, though we don't know yet where we're going. (Ah, ambiguity— my good friend!) Deb keeps looking at other jobs, so we don't know whether we'll be staying here or going elsewhere. So far, though, nothing is panning-out. It's still hard to believe that anyone would reject Dr. Fabian, with her credentials and experience; but losing the Connecticut job was another reality slap. The transgender issue is definitely limiting us.

7/9/12: Deb and I were alone for the weekend, after the departure of our 4th of July guests. It was a really sweet time for the two of us, though we're still not making love. I don't think we have since the transition. I notice it's the <u>idea</u> of not being sexual that bugs me; of going for months without that physical intimacy. But it seems bizarre, that I <u>think</u> we should make love, even though the desire (for both of us) seems entirely absent. Something in me says this is a good thing, that we no longer seem to have a desire for sex. Another part keeps saying, "That's ridiculous! You should be making love!"

We talk about it, agreeing that maybe we ought to give it a try. Deb says, "Let's schedule it," but that's as far as it goes. Neither of us initiates anything, and the odd thing is that this seems okay (except for my judgment of it). Such a strange process! I'd like to develop a Jack Kerouac attitude: "I don't know; I don't care; and it doesn't matter anyway." That's tolerance for ambiguity, detachment, and acceptance, all rolled into one lucid statement!

7/10/12: Three weeks from today we need to be out of this condo. We've found a house to rent and I'm actually excited. We <u>love</u> this house! This year is turning into one transition after another, so it's a good thing I tend to appreciate newness and adventure. Time to practice the "let go and let God" routine…and get some boxes packed! My "Daily Word" says, "Spirit within guides my steps and lights my way," and I'm trusting this. This move is simply another tiny drop in the tiny bucket of my tiny lifetime; just another little unexpected glitch.

7/25/12: It's moving week and I've declared that all will go easily and gracefully. We're making trips to the new house every evening, and the movers will be here in a couple of days to take over the task. They'll finish getting everything out of the condo & into the house. Was I <u>really</u> doing this just a year ago, while preparing for David's transition, too?

8/9/12: Yea! I'm back at the cabin, ready to spend as much time here as I can before the season ends. As far as I'm concerned, we're settled enough in the new house, and I've made writing my #1 priority again. My self-discipline—getting my butt in the chair—needs tweaking, but my commitment endures and I continue to love the writing, once I get to it. I need to have my High Self step in and take charge; I'm just too good at letting things slide. I have a commitment and I'm letting myself down when I don't honor it. I <u>will</u> finish this book!

8/18/12: Deb came to the lake last night and it's good to be together again. Unbelievably, though, after we've been apart for awhile, I still forget it's not David who'll be joining me. I feel surprised, disappointed, to see Deborah standing on the dock, waiting for me to pick her up. Is this more denial? Magical thinking? It's odd and surprising that this is still going on. It's the same way I felt when she came to St. Augustine last February, as if a close woman friend were visiting; or when I returned to Gardner in March, wanting my husband to greet me. It still doesn't feel quite right to me. Will it ever? I remember thinking once: *Will there come a time when we'll forget she was once a man?* I doubt it, but how can I possibly know?

8/26/12: Deb's on-call in Gardner and we had tickets to a concert in New Hampshire last night, so I took a friend instead. While using the women's room at this outdoor venue, I wondered how Deb would have managed. There were long, slow lines during intermissions and many stalls inside the bathroom, as well as an attendant. Would D have passed well enough, or would there have been trouble? God! There are so many things to consider since this transition—like where she'll be comfortable and, more importantly, safe. It's actually <u>illegal</u> for her to use a women's restroom in Massachusetts, and I wonder about NH. Their motto is "live free or die." Does this extend to transsexuals, too? As I consider this, I notice how these thoughts continue to pervade my life. So, I'm now declaring today a "gender-free day," without any more attention to transitions of the gender kind, or anything else related to my spouse's changes. That feels liberating!

8/30/12: I'm considering the discrimination lawsuit, contemplating how much of what now happens in our lives relates to my transsexual mate's becoming a woman. I'm bothered by the energy I'm putting into it, because it just shouldn't matter! Deb is a remarkable human being with a beautiful soul, not to mention brilliance and skill as a surgeon. I can see the comfort in maintaining an "acceptable" façade, though comfort was the <u>last</u> thing David felt in living the lie of manhood. Why should it have to be so hard for her to exist in her new form?

I must remember all that I've endured in my life; the strength that got me through those things. David has chosen to create this complexity (despite having no choice about the internal situation) and I'm colluding with it. This struggle to be accepted, to be treated with respect and fairness—I suppose it could go on for the rest of our lives, to some degree. It will follow us and challenge others, thereby challenging us. Are there ways to be at peace with this? Will we find them?

9/1/12: Deb arrived at the lake last night and we met for dinner, our Friday night summer custom: I go by boat, she arrives by car, and we meet at our favorite restaurant on the bay. The waitresses there know us pretty well now and greet us with the same kindness and support that we get in Massachusetts. They invariably ask how things are going and seem to want to cheer us on. Despite this pleasantry, by the time we got to the cabin last evening, I felt aggravated to have Deb here. It's an unpleasant feeling and I'm wondering about it. I suppose writing about the transition for five days straight stirs up all the emotions I was having at the time I'm writing about, making it real again. I'm living it twice. This makes sense, but it seems unfair on my part, especially since I've had the whole week here to myself. I want this to be respite for Debby, too.

Again, I'm bothered by the lack of attraction I feel for my mate. Making love at the cabin was always so delicious; I really miss it. We're always affectionate when we're here alone, but I have no desire to be sexual with Deb, and it's hard to talk about it. It makes us both so sad. Besides, she knows how I feel; it makes no sense to keep digging around in it. Maybe we'll have a session or two with my therapist, to sort this out. OMG—our lives are so complicated right now. Is it any wonder that I run to the cabin and want it all to myself? I must remember the impermanence and unimportance of all this, in the grand scheme of things.

9/25/12: Back to my writing this morning with a tedious task ahead. I'm working on the "Telling the Family" chapter again and have heard from one of the kids that he wants to be taken out of the book entirely. He was unhappy with what I'd said about him. I've decided to rewrite the whole damn thing and remove all the kids' names. I certainly don't want to have to deal with this five more times! I'm struck, once again, by how challenging it seems for our boys, and for men in general, to deal with this. I think the rules of being a male are so firmly implanted in them that the thought of becoming a woman is just too outrageous.

9/30/12: I've been in Tampa this weekend for my 45th high school reunion and it's been a blast! It seems that time continues to blur the lines that once divided and separated us. I had many wonderful conversations, realizing that, at age sixty-three, most of us have been through something big in our lives. I talked about the transition a lot. In fact, I had put it on Facebook before the event, so it would be old news when I got here. Most folks seemed curious, interested; and they were kind and concerned for me.

I discovered that one old friend is losing her husband to early-onset Alzheimer's. This seems far worse than my loss. I still have a functioning spouse. Another friend who'd never responded to the transition letter last year told me, "I feel so sorry for you." This is a projection on her part; I certainly don't need people feeling sorry for me. But it seemed apparent that she doesn't want to be around me anymore. Surprisingly, a third friend, one that I thought would be averse to the transition, is totally supportive. There's just no predicting who'll go which way.

10/2/12: I got home from Tampa last night and met Deb for dinner on the way back from the airport. It's good to be home, though I realize again that it's my <u>husband</u> I miss when we're apart, even though there's no husband to be had. When I'm away from home, the whole situation seems surreal. It's as if I'm telling a story about somebody else and will, of course, be returning to David. But this is my reality now: My husband no longer exists. How many times do I have to say this to believe it?

Twice, while talking to friends in Tampa, I was in tears as I told our story (could be why one feels sorry for me). I told Deb about all of this and she's as supportive as ever, offering whatever I think might help. What would help is to wake up one day and have all of this gone, lying next to a husband who's happy to be a man! I suppose this is the way David used to wish he'd wake up and he'd be a woman, or that his longing to be female would have disappeared. This thinking is painful & useless, but the feelings are certainly real.

I've decided to call the Concord therapist for an appointment. Maybe a few sessions will help me address this sadness that keeps resurfacing. It's been almost a year since the transition; I'd think I'd be over my wishful thinking by now.

10/3/12: Fantasia Fair is in a couple of weeks and I have a presentation to prepare. I signed-up last year, not even sure what I'd planned to say, but I thought I'd have a finished book to offer. Well, maybe next year. I'll probably read excerpts and talk about how I've supported the transition—and I'll be as honest as I am in my writing (of course). I wonder how many wives I'll scare and alienate. I know this is their worst nightmare.

The other thing to tackle is writing the letter that will mark the completion of our first year as Leslie and Deborah, a follow-up to last year's letter, announcing the transition. I've decided to end the book with it. Otherwise, how will I ever wrap it up? This story will go on and on...

10/4/12: God! What a day yesterday! I'd sent a section of my "Telling the Family" chapter to my brother and his wife, wanting to make sure it's accurate. From the way they've reacted, you'd think I made the whole thing up. But it's basically the saved e-mails among the four of us, from just after she'd told him about the transition. They were incredibly upset about what I'd said in my narrative, and I had the most disturbing phone conversation with my sister-in-law. (I guess she's the peacemaker; my brother didn't call.) I really lost it with her—crying, yelling...watching myself as I blew-up and fell-apart on the phone, hardly believing what I was saying! I finally had to hang up, though I did have the wherewithal to end with, "I love you, but I can't talk about this anymore."

I'm putting this chapter aside for now. It's an essential component of the book, but it's just too controversial. I'd had the exchange with my son already, then took all the kids' names out of the book. This is just more aggravation and pain. Either folks are uncomfortable seeing themselves exposed like this, or I'm misrepresenting them, and I don't want to do that. If it weren't so disturbing, it would be funny! My whole objective in sending these excerpts was to make sure I wasn't offending anyone, and I truly didn't think I was. I've had it with this chapter for now. I'm moving-on to the next section and will come back to this one later.

10/6/12: Deb's continued to look at other jobs and is still having trouble with the responses (or lack thereof). Recruiters don't return her calls or respond to her CV, once they realize she was a man; and this is obvious when anyone looks at her past credentials. It's frustrating and bizarre, but it's becoming a common occurrence. I think she needs to accept that finding another job and starting over again will never be what it was when she was David. And we both need to be grateful for the amazing acceptance of the Gardner community and the success of her existing practice, and settle back in here.

10/7/12: My brother and his wife have sent e-mails, explaining their objections to my writing, but I just can't bring myself to read them right now. It's been too hurtful, on top of all the emotions of the situation itself. This reminds me of a divorce situation, with everyone having opinions and judgments, and of losing beloved people because a couple decides to split-up. It doesn't have to be like this, but there's nothing I can do to control it.

10/11/12: We've closed the cabin for another year and I already miss my solitude. It's hard to return to this other routine—the more complicated mornings of two people arising and dealing with our AM tasks, and my inevitable (it seems) re-involvement in Deborah's clothing choices and hair.

I sent my brother and sister-in-law an e-card this morning with a dove of peace and a message of love and positive expectations. I'd come across the Rumi quote: "…if you have any sense, my friend, don't plant anything but love," and this is my intention. I'm glad I've put that family chapter on-hold. I never expected anything like this when I began my writing, but I know that the right answers will come to light in time.

10/12/12: Today is my therapy appointment and it's timely. After the blow-up with my sister-in-law, I really need to vent. I must also explore what's occurring inside me, relative to Deb's and my relationship: It's morphing, and I guess I've known this was inevitable. D tells me, "I'm so in love with you," and I recognize my deep love for her. But I no longer feel "in-love," in the old familiar ways. I miss the passion and appreciation of our differences as a man and a woman—what I've always loved in my relationships. This may not mean that anything needs to be done; it just needs to be acknowledged for what it is. We shall see what comes up in my therapy session. "Daily Word" reminds me: "Grace is ever-available and always sufficient. I am fully supported by the divine." I love those reminders.

10/16/12: Well, it was a help to have the therapist's undivided attention and compassionate response, though I realize again that I've become my own best therapist. One session helps me verbalize what's bugging me and get myself on the path to resolution. (Ha! That's a laugh! Resolution sounds so finite and complete; as if we can just wrap up this whole affair and consider it done!) I think my spiritual guides have as much to offer as a therapist, and Thomas Merton never lets me down: "…keep still and let [God] do some work." Yes; I could do this more often, though keeping still has never been one of my strong points. I know that time will help me deal with the loss of passion and ease these absurd emotional fluctuations.

Deb was on-call in New Hampshire over the weekend [she does this monthly], and I stayed at home. Now she's back and it's really sweet to have her here with me. A therapist asked me, long ago, "What is it that you love about David?" I think I could answer this much better now, in spite of the transition and absence of David. What I love is looking forward to the return of my pal and companion; the love of my life. And I love our familiarity with each other; our twenty years of history, and surviving divorces and the childhoods of six kids. I love the way my spouse listens to me, understands me (or tries to); her willingness to stick with me when we have a problem and help find a resolution. I love that, for so long, she told me, "I'll stop this if it means losing you;" and that we laugh at the same things, including ourselves and each other. I love that I can tell Deb anything, no matter how hard it might be. There is so much to love; it's good to look at the ways. Methinks this is a good sign!

10/17/12: We're on the Cape now, for Fantasia Fair. I'll be presenting in two hours and I'm excited. I can finally enjoy sharing our story and my thoughts and feelings about the transition—quite a switch from last year, when I was completely worn out and fed-up with talking about it. It's so good to be with this crowd again. These are the folks who understand what we're going through.

10/18/12: The presentation was great (if I do say so myself). The response to my book excerpts was good and we had some wonderful discussion. I loved presenting to the intimate group that attended my talk, feeling comfortable and supported. Deb couldn't take much time off, but drove the four hours each way and stayed for two nights. She wanted to see our dear friends, and to be in the room for my presentation—one of the many ways she supports me.

10/23/12: It's time to finish the up-date letter, marking the one year anniversary of Deb's coming-out. The writing is heartening, as I review the miracles that have taken place over the past year. It feels good to be composing something about how well we are doing in this new life of ours.

I still wonder about us. But, as I told Debby in May, I'm committed—though I'm not really sure what it is I'm committed to! A marriage, or what? It's a friendship, for sure; a partnership that's clearly meant to be. It's a love I'd never known before David, yet somehow knew existed, though it's now beyond anything I'd imagined. And it's grown through our twenty-five years together. It's rich and satisfying, safe, and rewarding.

Hey, it just is what it is, and I'm learning to accept what it is with grace and gratitude, regardless of what anyone else may think. A favorite quote from Julian of Norwich comes to mind, so simple, so true: "All shall be well, and all shall be well, and all manner of thing shall be well." This touches and comforts me, and I know that for us, "... all manner of thing shall be well."

Deborah & Leslie Fabian

To be what we are, and to become what we are capable of becoming, is the only end of life. –Robert Louis Stevenson

October, 2012

Dear Ones:

It has now been a year since David became Deborah and it seems that an update is in order. The nature of Deborah's and my relationship continues to transform and defies definition or naming, so we simply don't bother to label it. Understandably, our process has been challenging at times, though our love has not abated. To see Deborah's joy at finally being true to herself is a most gratifying experience for me—and I couldn't feel more loved by her.

The response of the medical staff to Dr. Deborah's emergence has been overwhelmingly positive. Many of her colleagues have expressed appreciation for the information she has shared, as it enhances their understanding of transgender patients. Deb's orthopedic practice continues unaltered, with patients consulting and having their surgeries performed by her. As we had hoped, folks recognize that changing genders has not changed her medical and surgical skills. And, of course, her happiness enhances every aspect of her life.

Praise for Deborah's courage has been abundant. Many people have shared heart-warming stories of healing old wounds with family and friends, as a result of reading the touching letter sent to patients last fall. Patients and staff have revealed their own struggles in dealing with transgender, lesbian, or gay family members; they speak of their gratitude for Deborah's inspiration. The community continues to embrace us and we are moved beyond words by the miraculous acceptance of this change.

Deb's parents were told of the transition shortly after it occurred, and my mother-in-law spent her first day with Deborah last November. When asked what she thought of her new daughter, Dottie said, "I've decided to love the person on the inside." Though she'd never had a clue that her son was so unhappy with his gender, Mom has been curious and open about the transition. At ninety-six, she is incredibly supportive and is even writing about the experience. We are blessed by her caring and acceptance.

Sadly, Deb's father Bob passed-away in March, so we'll never know his long-term response. Mostly, he seemed confused about it. Among his last words to his former son were, "You're David, aren't you? You need a haircut!"

All of our children and their partners, bless their hearts, are sticking with us. They all seem to realize that this transition and Debby's happiness trump the difficulties of accepting a parent in so different a form. They have risen above any fears and concerns they initially had, and we are proud of them and so very gratified.

I stopped seeing clients a couple of years ago and began going south in the winters. Writing has become my passion and full-time work, and it's been a great source of relief and release for me as I've navigated these uncharted waters. I am nearing completion of a book about all of this with the working title *My Husband's a Woman Now: A Shared Journey of Transition and Love*. This book has emerged as our love story and I'm hoping for its publication soon. Perhaps you'll enjoy reading about our amazing experience.

Please stay in touch, if you are so inclined.

With our love and appreciation to all,

Leslie

Bless you, we love you—Be peaceful, be well!

PART FOUR
LESSONS LEARNED

March 2012

We do not receive wisdom, we must discover it for ourselves, after a journey through the wilderness which no one else can make for us, which no one can spare us, for our wisdom is the point of view from which we must come at last to regard the world. –Marcel Proust

∞

CHAPTER TWENTY-FOUR
WHAT THIS EXPERIENCE HAS TAUGHT ME

1. LEARNING TO LIVE WITH CONTRADICTION AND THE UNKNOWN IS ESSENTIAL

During the time leading-up to the transition, I was never certain whether our marriage would last or how I'd traverse the changes that were occurring daily. I wondered whether I was nuts to be going along with this. I was also profoundly aware that, while supporting my husband's change because I loved him and wanted him to be happy, I was relinquishing my desire to remain married to the *man* I loved. The fact is, life is rife with ambiguity and paradox.

I had to make room for holding two or more conflicting thoughts or feelings at the same time. When my husband's breasts appeared, I reacted. I felt unable to continue touching him, even though I had known that this physical change would occur. But it did not make sense to me; this was still my beloved. I found that these conflicted thoughts and feelings eased with the passage of time.

2. IT IS CRUCIAL *NEVER* TO SAY "NEVER"

I'd begun learning this when I first became involved with David, having proclaimed that I could *never* be the "other woman." And I'm reasonably certainly that, years ago, I'd *never* have supported my husband's transition. How many times have I caught myself saying *"never,"* only to have to back-track?

3. THE SOLID FOUNDATION IN OUR RELATIONSHIP CAN HELP US ENDURE ALMOST ANYTHING

Building and maintaining a loving, supportive marriage has always been a requirement for us. We share a deep well of empathy and mutual support. I was encouraging my beloved to do something that, in the future, I might not choose to live with. This required strength, clarity, and the sacrifice of what I most wanted vs. what s/he most wanted. I could not have done this without the firm base we'd established.

My spouse understood how difficult the transition was for me, though I sometimes needed to remind him that I was struggling. Because of our solidity, I was able to forgive his forgetting, and he could accept my reminders.

Redefining our relationship has been necessary and is an on-going process. I doubt that this would be possible without the strength of our marriage. All the reasons that I loved David still exist with Deborah. And while I may always miss David, I have Debby to love, and to love me. Yes; it's different; but the loving hasn't gone away, the history is still ours, and the connection has endured.

4. A BASIC PERSONALITY WILL REMAIN THE SAME, DESPITE TRANSITIONING

Regardless of how supportive I've been, no matter how much my spouse has changed or how happy she is now, there will still be old, challenging behaviors and issues. Just as the good remains, so does the not-so-good. If a relationship is not solid and loving to begin with, its demise cannot be blamed entirely on a transition or anything else that occurs.

5. BEING TRUE TO MYSELF MEANS MANY THINGS

I was honoring my intuition when I told my husband, "I think it's time for you to talk to an endocrinologist." I learned that I am sometimes my own best coach and therapist; that I can often trust my own instincts to guide me.

I knew that I would not allow the transition to destroy my own happiness. And I've always been committed to being completely honest about what is true for me, even though what I choose may be hurtful to another. I realized that I sometimes need to stand my ground and be firm on what I want or need—though not out of anger, resentment, or retaliation.

We both found that we must be "thick-skinned." As we went along, we prepared to face judgment, hatred, confusion, discrimination, rudeness, rejection. It's so important to remember that others thoughts, words, and deeds are about them and their view of the world, not about me or us.

I discovered that being true to myself and to my mate necessitates a willingness to let go of some relationships—even with family members, if they are unable to accept us. This would extend to relinquishing my marriage, if I determined that it was no longer working for me after the transition.

6. TAKING CARE OF MYSELF WAS, IS, AND ALWAYS WILL BE CRUCIAL

I knew that I must be clear, honest, and gentle with myself, as well as with my spouse and others, bearing in mind that if I don't care for myself, I can't adequately take care of anyone else.

My emotions were unpredictable and surprising. I might be having a great day, then find myself disbelieving and distressed with what was occurring in our lives, feeling enraged or in tears, perhaps wanting to run away. As with any traumatic event, I went through all the stages of grief, which came and went at random. This was another way in which I learned to expect the unexpected and the necessity of taking really good care of myself.

I honored the need to seek and use whatever was helpful for dealing with such enormous change, such as journaling, writing, therapy, coaching, friends, solitude, and being in nature. I used what has helped in the past and found new methods for assistance. I knew the value and comfort of finding and spending time with others like us, such as support groups and Fantasia

Fair. And I found that distractions are helpful and service to others can change the focus and fulfill me.

I needed to recognize when I was being controlling and acknowledge that it was undoubtedly from feeling so *out-of-control* in my life. It was essential to talk with someone neutral who would validate my feelings, assist, and support me. And it helped to remember that imagination can run wild and be misleading. In actuality, I can imagine the best as readily as I can imagine the worst.

It behooved me to keep addressing the following: *What's in this for me? What will I be losing if I give up my marriage? What are the benefits of being married to this person, regardless of his/her gender?*

7. VULNERABILITY, THOUGH RISKY, CAN BUILD CONNECTION TO OTHERS

I watched as audiences and congregations warmed to my spouse when she told them of her life-long struggle. They responded with empathy and kindness. It was good for us as a couple, too, when we were vulnerable and took risks together, especially speaking to groups as a team. This built our connection, mutual support, and ability to stand in our Truth. However…

8. FEELING HAPPY AND OPTIMISTIC DOES NOT NEGATE THE NEED TO BE PRACTICAL, REALISTIC, AND MINDFUL OF THE NEED FOR ALTERNATIVE PLANS AND OPTIONS

There's no predicting outcomes. Sometimes nothing we'd planned went the way we had hoped. We needed to expect the unexpected with practically everything. It's helpful to remember that smooth sailing never lasts—nor do choppy waters.

Reality can sometimes be tough to take. There were unpleasant incidents as well as heart-warming reactions. Some of those whom we thought would reject Deborah accepted her; and some whom we thought would accept her rejected her.

I became wary of blind trust. Simply because we have integrity and are honest doesn't mean that others have these qualities. We had discovered this time after time with the job search, and certainly with the withdrawal of the position at the Connecticut Hospital.

Our "devil's advocates" had worthy observations and viewpoints to offer. I came to value listening to what others had to say and carefully considered their input, even when one or both of us disliked the advice.

It became essential to discuss practically everything and reach accord with one another. We needed to negotiate agreements and honor them—especially regarding safety, rationality, mutuality, and wise choices.

Hoping the transgenderism would go away was as irrational as thinking my skin color might change. This is magical thinking and it needs to be recognized for what it is, despite the temptation to fantasize.

9. NOTICE WHEN MY THOUGHTS AND OPINIONS ARE COMING FROM MY EGO, RATHER THAN FROM MY LOVING HEART AND A STRONG SENSE OF SELF

I needed to address my reactions, particularly when others focused entirely on David's transition, with no recognition of my role in it or how it was affecting me. I felt angry and hurt when this occurred and worked at doing whatever it took to move beyond the reaction and take care of myself.

I realized that it's not a reflection on me if Deborah doesn't do things the way I want her to. This is a paradox: My *ego* wants her to follow my suggestions, while it's my *ego* that allows me to feel secure and okay, if she is judged for something I think she should change!

10. IT'S IMPORTANT TO BE PREPARED TO TAKE LEGAL ACTION

Job recruiters began vanishing after being told of the impending transition. It is apparently an unfortunate fact that, in our current society, someone unusual must be prepared to defend the right to hold a job, despite being eminently qualified. David wisely hired an attorney in Connecticut to guide us through the process with the job there and, unfortunately, this proved to be necessary.

11. HOLDING RESENTMENT DOES NOT SERVE ME

Forgiveness is a requirement, in order to live and feel as I desire. It has been crucial to bear in mind that most people are uninformed and fearful of transgender issues. I aimed to do my best to educate and forgive them their ignorance, reactions, and judgments; to remember that, no matter how much they may have loved and respected us, some are not able to deal with this. I would forgive the folks who didn't seem to notice how this transition was changing and affecting my life. I'd also forgive myself, my spouse, and everybody else. Doing this was for me!

*Gratitude lifts us, like angels, above the cares
that weight us to the earth.* –Anonymous

∽

ACKNOWLEDGEMENTS

THROUGHOUT THE WRITING OF THIS BOOK and David's transition to Deborah, there have been countless kind souls who've encouraged me, supported me, and—most importantly—loved me. There is no possible way I'd have stuck with this task without the generous, enduring sustenance of my dear friends, family, and community. Thank you, each and all!

I also want my thanks "out there" to the professor at Boston College (whose name I no longer remember) who wrote on one of my graduate school papers, "You are a gifted writer." You have no idea how that one short statement has helped me to maintain the belief that I might be!

And then there's my professional support team, beginning with Judy Weigle—book shepherd par excellence. She's been a guiding light for two years, directing, correcting, editing, rarely coddling me (except in those moments when I needed a tender touch), cracking the whip when needed, and always nudging me on as a writer. I owe her an enormous debt of gratitude.

Dear Judy, you have been one of the essential components of this process. And beyond your brilliant expertise, guidance, and encouragement, there is the laughter and true friendship you have lavished on me. You've been everything from a mother hen to a tigress in this process. Thank you from the bottom of my heart for taking me on and sticking with me, from your coast to mine. And bunches more thanks for our one meeting in Los Angeles, for dinner and the trip to the candy store!

I am so grateful for the therapists, teachers, spiritual guides, facilitators, and others who have helped me to heal and grow in ways I might never have discovered, had I been going it alone.

To Niela Miller, whose creation of the Women's Floating Circle (1986-2004) brought my beloved to me. And for unequaled guidance, encouragement, brilliance, and friendship—there's no one like Niela!

My life coach, Janet Parker, is one incredibly wise woman and friend. She has never failed in assisting me to get my life back on course, especially when I've felt like a stranger in a strange land. Thank you, Janet, for decades of guidance.

My heart-felt gratitude goes to Maureen Streff, Claude Marchessault, and Dennis Reynolds, for listening, caring, and invariably knowing what to say—or not to say! And thanks to Meg Striepe for affirming me and my process in many ways.

To Robert Fritz, his DMA training, and his book *The Path of Least Resistance*, all of which compelled me to begin creating the life that I most desired.

To John-Roger (J-R) and the Insight Seminars, which he founded—and to Russell Bishop, who created them—for promoting ever-deeper levels of loving, acceptance, wonder, health, satisfaction, and joy. My heart is filled with enduring appreciation and reverence for J-R, my spiritual teacher and guide. Immense gratitude to the remarkable facilitators, especially Janet, Maryanne, Martha, Razz, Terry, Candace, and Stu.

To the Movement of Spiritual Inner Awareness [MSIA] and my fellow travelers, particularly John-Roger (again—always, all ways), John Morton, and my New England community. You help to lift me out of the mundane into the sacred, and to remember who I really am. The blessings of ease and grace are found here.

To Harville Hendrix, Helen Hunt, and the remarkable Imago therapists with whom David/Deborah and I have worked to Find the Love That We Want with each other.

To Joyce and Barry Vissell, guides extraordinaire in practical loving and spiritual connection—and the Hawaiian explorers who led us to the lava at the end of the cliff. (I'm sure there's a metaphor there somewhere!)

To Doug Kraft, the wonderful UU minister who coached and married us in 1991, an integral part of our story.

To the fabulous, annual Fantasia Fair and its organizers, participants, events, and workshops, with extra-special kudos to Sandra Cole. Her kindness and understanding of the wives' and partners' unique position in the lives of the transgendered is a gift to us all.

To John Harrington, MD, everyone at Henry Heywood and Athol Hospitals, and the people of Gardner and Athol, Massachusetts, and surrounding areas. You've taken us beyond our wildest dreams, providing on-going miracles of respect, acceptance, kindness, and grace. Thank you so much for loving us!

To Jenny Stevens, a dear friend who's cheered me on all along the way, as well as reading my manuscript and providing invaluable feedback. And to Snowden McFall, another long-time friend who read, advised, and encouraged me with generosity and assurance.

To David Flemming, MD, whose creativity with a camera and computer editing skills are exceeded only by his (and Joy's) caring friendship and support.

To the dear, loving congregants of the Unitarian Universalist Society of Gardner—and to members of UU churches everywhere—for your loving hearts, open minds, and for always seeking the Truth.

To a mother-in-law whose generosity of spirit continues to amaze us. You are a wonder, Mom!

To our six precious children and your exceptional spouses and partners, for showing us what being a family really means.

To the family members whose bounteous caring and love have exceeded all expectations and hope.

And to my darling Debby: Practically speaking, for a great story that begged to be written! For your devotion to us. And for your brilliance, courage, and a new-found joy that renders you nearly incapable of anger, frustration, or blame. What a pleasure that is! You, My Love, fill me with wonder and gratitude!

And finally, thank you, Spirit—
for a life beyond compare. I live in awe!

AFTERWORD

∞

By Deborah Rae Fabian, MD

I'VE BEEN TOLD THAT, in transitioning, one needs to be willing and prepared to lose everything and everyone in his or her life. Unfortunately, I believe that this is true. What we transsexuals have done or are doing, the way in which we live, will not work for everyone.

I propose that there is much we can do to lessen the likelihood of losses. To others who are facing this transsexual challenge, I suggest giving conscious thought to *all* existing relationships. I have found that every one of mine has had its own transition, of sorts.

As I moved through this change, I explained to others what I was doing and what to expect during the process. I gave them opportunities to ask questions and give opinions. I wanted to do whatever I could to maintain the relationships that I value, for if I had lost them, my transition would not have brought me the joy that it has. I felt that it was up to me to be open and honest with everyone, and I'm blessed that only a few individuals have reacted negatively. Even this has not resulted in a significant loss of relationships.

I'm aware that I am fortunate to be in a profession and setting with open-minded colleagues. My office staff has accepted me, and I trust it's not simply because they are my employees. The support for me has been miraculous! I think that one reason for this is that I shared with many people in the early stages of my transition. I sought their advice and support.

Of course, for the hospital and office staffs, even our friends, it has largely been a matter of learning to choose the right pronoun. For my patients it has been a matter of trust and faith in my abilities. For Leslie, it was obviously an enormous alteration of nearly everything in our lives. So, to others considering transitioning, I recommend going beyond the question *Can I do it?* and asking the following: *How can I make sure that my partner feels loved? What do I wish to bring to this relationship that can help it to grow and deepen? Can I commit myself to loving my mate unconditionally, as I am asking of her?*

My need to keep Leslie in my life, as my wife, was of paramount importance. I cared enough to attempt to give up my dream, if following-through meant losing her. I'm actually not certain I could have done it, but the value I place on our love and relationship would have made me try.

Every day, I make an effort to devote energy to Leslie and to our relationship, to keep it strong. Since my transition, our relationship has changed, without a doubt. But we both now recognize and celebrate a deeper level of loving—a love of that spiritual self, that inner person, described by philosophers and spiritualists.

Jennifer Finney Boylan, transsexual and author of *She's Not There,* prayed to be saved by love. That same prayer has been answered for me: My wife is still my wife. I'm certain that, on many levels, Leslie's love has saved me. And I am incredibly blessed that she has remained my wife and life partner.

The initial title for this book was *It's My Transition Too.* Perhaps all transgender individuals might reflect on this concept. I needed to transition to save my life—or, finally, to live with myself in peace. Leslie got pulled along (although she did some pushing, too). She did this because she cared about my happiness and wanted me to be myself, what I always knew myself to be. How can I do anything less for her? My wish for her is to experience the life that she chooses and to become all that she is, all that she would like to become. This is, after all,

HER TRANSITION, TOO!

GLOSSARY OF TERMS

∞

Androgynous – Appearing neither clearly masculine nor clearly feminine; possessing both female and male characteristics.

Facial Feminization Surgery – Reconstructive surgical procedures which alter typically male facial features to more closely resemble typical female facial features in size and shape.

Gender Identity – The innate sense of gender that an individual intrinsically feels which may or may not be harmonious with his or her physical gender. Note that the vast majority of people feel congruency with their physical gender.

Incongruent Gender Identity – Having a sense of gender that is incompatible with one's physical gender characteristics.

Sex Reassignment Surgery (or Gender Correction Surgery, Gender Reassignment Surgery, Genital Reconstruction Surgery, Sex Affirmation Surgery, or Sex Realignment Surgery) – The procedures by which a person's physical appearance and the function of their existing sexual characteristics are surgically altered to resemble those of the other sex.

Sexual Orientation – The sexual attraction that a person feels towards another person, based on the gender of the other person. This is distinct from gender identity.

Transgender(ed) – An umbrella term that applies to any person who has a gender identity that is incongruous with his or her sex, or who sometimes enjoys appearing as the opposite sex.

Transsexual – A person who has a gender identity that is opposite his or her birth sex and who strongly feels he or she should live fully as a member of the gender with which he or she identifies. A non-operative transsexual is a person who lives his or her life as a member of the opposite gender, without ever undergoing or planning to undergo surgery.

Definitions are from the Internet and *Transitions: A Guide to Transitioning for Transsexuals and Their Families* by Mara Drummond.

A SHORT LIST OF ADDITIONAL READING

My Brother My Sister by Molly Haskell: One woman's experience in learning to accept her brother's transition to female.

She's Not There by Jennifer Finney Boylan: An excellent personal story of transition by a professor of English at Colby College.

Transitions: A Guide to Transitioning for Transsexuals and Their Families by Mara Drummond: Advice on how to proceed.

True Selves by Mildred Brown and Chloe Rounsley: A collection of stories, poetry, and precise information about the transgender phenomenon.

CPSIA information can be obtained
at www.ICGtesting.com
Printed in the USA
BVHW030053190219
540623BV00001B/42/P